The Heart of the King

A Devotional Commentary

on Psalm 119

The Heart of the King

A Devotional Commentary

on Psalm 119

Ron Auch

New Leaf Press

First Edition
January 1995

ISBN: 0-89221-278-0
Library of Congress Number: 94-68844

Cover by Multnomah Graphics, Portland, Oregon.

All Scripture quotations are from the New International Version of the Bible.

Dedication

This book is dedicated to the "faithful few" who met with me for over a year to have "Lunch with Jesus." During our time together we prayed and meditated over the 119th Psalm, which was truly the birthplace of this book.

May God continue to bless their lives.

Acknowledgments

A heartfelt "thank you" must go to several people who had a part in the completion of this book.

First, I must thank John Cronce for his help once again. John has helped on each of my books, and what he does is no small thing.

Jo Ann Rodriguez spent many hours entering this information into the computer, as did my sister-in-law, Geri Auch.

Finally, I must give a special thanks to Sue Smolinski; her son Todd; and my wife, Lou Ann, who spent countless hours doing the final editing. Without the help of all of these people, this book would not have been possible.

Introduction

The title of this book, *The Heart of the King,* refers to King David. It was said of David that he had a heart that sought out the heart of God (1 Sam. 13:14). Psalm 119 reveals his heart in a way that no other portion of Scripture does. This entire Psalm is a prayer that expresses David's innermost feelings about his God. If we follow the admonitions in this Psalm, we will develop into spiritual beings. David was a spiritual man, and the things he prayed were an expression of that.

Using this Psalm as a prayer began to interest me after reading an article by Rex B. Andrews from the 1960 issue of *Feed My Lambs* in which I found he had a practice of praying through it every day. If a person were to pray this every day, he would find himself going through some very transforming things. To read/pray* through it, we will express things we do not ordinarily express. It teaches us to say the things the Holy Spirit wants us to say. Though I am not suggesting we always, only, pray this Psalm, all we will ever need to pray is in its root form here.

We may have difficulty praying something that may not seem true of us at this particular time. In Psalm 119:8, for instance, we read, "I will obey your decrees. . . ." We may ask, "What good can there be in saying, 'I will obey,' when I continually disobey?" By praying this, it becomes more and more clear that we aren't as spiritual as we thought, and that we actually need God to help us. Remember that by praying this Psalm, we are praying what the Holy Spirit wants us to pray. Pray it as it is, even though we may not have fully accomplished what it says yet.

This Psalm furnishes something that we cannot find anywhere else. It brings us into a desire for God, and it is given in a way that only God can express. As Rex Andrews said, "It contains a prayer for quickening. 'Quicken me according to thy word,' is a common phrase. The power of the Psalmist's utterance is somewhat dimmed by the old English word 'quicken.' That word is hardly ever used in our present speech in its primary directness." What the term "quicken" actually means in this Psalm is: "PUT ME TO LIFE." In this study, we will use the New International Version of the Bible, where instead of "quicken me," we will see the phrase, "preserve my life." In either case, it is asking God to put or bring life into you.

The words *word, law, statute, testimony, commandment, precept,* and *judgment* cover the whole range of what the Word of God is. Rex Andrews' definition of these words will be used in studying this Psalm.

To use this Psalm as a prayer, we will be involving ourselves in devotional type praying. It is also a meditation.** These are the most important type of prayers there are because they develop intimacy with God. Devotional or meditative prayers are different from what we may be used to. This is internal prayer, not external. This type of praying causes us to go inward and to look at the intimacy of our relationship with God. In praying this Psalm, we will be going through what is called a "heart searching." It reveals the current condition of our own heart and shows us how much we need a heart like King David's.

Praying the 119th Psalm

There are 22 sections of Scripture in the 119th Psalm. Each section is 8 verses long. The subtitle at the beginning of each section is one of the letters in the Hebrew alphabet. For instance, the first section begins with the subtitle "Aleph." Aleph is the word for the first letter in the Hebrew alphabet. "Beth" is the subtitle for the second section. "Beth" is also the word for the second letter of the Hebrew alphabet, etc. These subtitles are found in most Bibles.

There are two ways we can effectively use this as a prayer. 1) Each day read/pray over one section of 8 verses. This could be done in an hour's time. It would prove to be an excellent way to spend an hour in prayer. The author suggests that we read the particular verse and the following commentary, then meditate on the verse for a few minutes. If we spend around 7 minutes on each verse, it will take close to an hour to go through one section. 2) Another approach would be to take one verse a day, and use this as a daily devotional. Obviously we would want to add this to our daily time of prayer because it would be difficult to spend an hour meditating on just one verse. This approach would take 176 days to go through the entire Psalm. May God bless you on your adventure!

*The term read/pray simply means to carefully and thoughtfully read the verse and then pray over it.

**Meditating on the Scriptures is done through simply repeating a verse over and over. This can be done verbally or in your mind. To meditate verbally or audibly you will keep yourself from daydreaming. Many of the promises for success in the Bible come through meditating on the Word of God. After you read the verse and commentary, then take the next few minutes to say the verse over and over while subconsciously keeping the commentary in mind.

Aleph

1. Blessed are they whose ways are blameless, who walk according to the law of the Lord.

Are you one of those who are "blessed" because all your ways are upright, with no hidden agendas? "There is a way that seems right to a man, but in the end it leads to death" (Prov. 14:12). The only way for our "way" to be blameless is to walk according to the law of the Lord.

What is the summation of the law of the Lord? Mercy. We can measure all our ways by that one standard. Will our way result in others being blessed? Only when we think in terms of mercy will we be blameless in all our ways. If we do everything for the sake of blessing others, no one can blame us for doing anything wrong. Do you understand what the result of most sin is? Sin is the deprivation of someone else. The reason sin hurts God is because of how our sin hurts those He loves.

The law of the Lord is mercy. In all that God does, He does it to have mercy on others. If a man murders another man, it is such a tragedy from God's perspective, because the murdered man no longer has the opportunity to be a recipient of the mercy of God. Whenever we sin, we rob someone else of the mercy of God. If a father or mother has a "way" in their life that is not blameless (a way full of self-centeredness), they deprive their own children of God's mercy.

To walk blamelessly, we must walk in mercy. It is the merciful who continue to receive mercy. We must understand that the will of God is mercy. It is God's desire to reveal His mercy to all people at all times; therefore, everything we do should be done in that light. To walk according to the law of the Lord is to do so with the intention of revealing God to others through having mercy on them.

As you meditate on this verse, ask God to show you all the ways of your heart that do not yet reflect Him.

2. Blessed are they who keep his statutes and seek him with all their heart.

A statute is a distinct law, an explicit law. There is no compromising a statute — it must be obeyed. Blessed are those who practice the fear of God to the point that they recognize there is no wavering when it comes to a statute.

The only way to develop unwavering obedience is through seeking God with all our heart. "Their heart is deceitful [divided], and now they must bear their guilt. . . ." Hosea 10:2 tells us that because the people of God did not have their hearts focused wholly on God, they did not seek Him wholly. Subsequently, they developed idols. Psalm 10:4 says, "In his pride the wicked does not seek him; in all his thoughts there is no room for God." The primary "idol" which causes us to not seek God is called *self.*

The people of Hosea's day had divided hearts. They could not fully seek God because they had more than one love. David tells us that the wicked, because of pride, do not seek God. Is there any greater occupation than self? When self becomes an idol, we are no longer able to keep God's statutes. It's only through the keeping of His statutes that we are able to seek Him with all our heart. To seek something with all our heart means our heart is surrendered to that thing. When we idolize self, our heart is not fully surrendered to God.

Whether self is an idol or not is determined by our prayer life. If we spend relatively small amounts of time in prayer, it's because we are not God-centered, we are self-centered. We cannot just have prayer in our life. All Christians have some type of prayer in their lives. We must have a prayer life, which, when defined, means someone whose very life comes from their time of prayer. That life is centered around prayer.

As you meditate on this verse, ask God to help you develop a heart that seeks Him wholly.

3. They do nothing wrong; they walk in his ways.

What a wonderful testimony to be said of anyone; they do nothing wrong! Is it your testimony? This whole Psalm is an inspection of the heart because the heart is the home of Jesus. Do you love Jesus enough to do nothing wrong? Do you love Him enough to walk in His ways? Our love of God is demonstrated by our obedience to Him. This is why rebellion is considered Satan worship. Rebellion is exactly the opposite of obedience. First Samuel 15:23 says, "For rebellion is like the sin of divination [witchcraft], and arrogance like the evil of idolatry. . . ." Those who have any rebellion in them cannot have the testimony "they do nothing wrong."

We are quick to quote John 15:7, "If you remain in me and my words remain in you, ask whatever you wish, and it will be given you." The word "remain" means to "live." If you live in Christ, or if Christ occupies your whole heart, you can ask whatever you wish in prayer and it will be given you. Some people live under the impression that since they are believers, they have the right to ask for anything they want from God and He must give it to them. There is a condition that must be met before we can simply ask for anything and have it given to us. The condition is to have the testimony that we do nothing wrong, we walk in His ways. To abide means more than just having Jesus in our heart. It is to live the life He lives. First John 2:6 puts it this way, "Whoever claims to live in him must walk as Jesus did."

To walk as Jesus walked means our flesh has been dealt with and it no longer controls our actions or desires. When a person is so submitted to God that he does nothing wrong, he then gains the privilege of asking for anything he wants and it will be granted to him. The idea behind this is that when our flesh has been dealt with, we will no longer ask for things that would be out of God's will.

As you meditate on this verse, ask God to help you gain the testimony that you do nothing wrong.

4. You have laid down precepts that are to be fully obeyed.

The word "precepts" covers what we generally mean by "instructions." Instructions are given as to what to do, when, how, etc. The precepts that God has laid down work to our benefit. We receive instructions in all things. If you are a secretary, you are to do your job according to God's precepts. The same is true of a plumber, a doctor, a lawyer, a preacher, etc. God will tell us how, when, and what. These are to be fully obeyed. If we will go through life obeying the instructions of God, then we can go through life fully expecting His blessings.

It is very similar to how a parent instructs a child. A parent has the child's best interest in mind. In Luke 11:11-13 we read, "Which of you fathers, if your son asks for a fish, will give him a snake instead? Or if he asks for an egg, will give him a scorpion? If you then, though you are evil, know how to give good gifts to your children, how much more will your Father in heaven give the Holy Spirit to those who ask him!"

We, being evil, know how to provide good things for our children. When we instruct our children, it's so we can provide good things for them. The same is true of our Heavenly Father but to a greater degree. When God lays down precepts, they are to be fully obeyed because they work to our benefit. God is not demanding obedience just because He has some kind of unquenchable ego. He wants obedience for the same reason a parent wants obedience. It is for the good of the child.

As you meditate on this verse, ask yourself if you really believe that everything God asks you to do is for your good.

5. Oh, that my ways were steadfast in obeying your decrees!

The word "decree" is the same as "statute." A statute is an explicit law. David's prayer was that his ways would be steadfast in obeying God's explicit laws. To be steadfast is to be adamant, firm, or resolute. It means it has been settled. There is no wavering in obedience to God's decrees.

We relate better to the apostle Paul in Romans 7:15, "I do not understand what I do. For what I want to do I do not do, but what I hate I do." The average Christian wants to be steadfast in his obedience to God but faces this constant conflict. Paul summed up his thoughts with this, "Thanks be to God — through Jesus Christ our Lord! So then, I myself in my mind am a slave to God's law, but in the sinful nature a slave to the law of sin" (Rom. 7:25). The battle for obedience is won or lost in the mind. If Paul had become a slave to the law of God in his mind, then he ultimately won the battle regardless of the struggle he may still have faced with his flesh.

Romans 12:2 says, "Do not conform any longer to the pattern of this world, but be transformed by the renewing of your mind. . . ." When we meditate on the Word of God (hide it in our heart), we begin to renew our mind. We are transformed through the renewing of our minds. When the mind is renewed, the flesh becomes subject to it. If we fail to take on the mind of Christ, our flesh continues to control our thoughts and actions.

How much time do you spend meditating on God's Word? Consider what is the greatest influence in your life. Whatever you spend the most time doing influences you the most. Do you spend more time in front of the television than you do in prayer and the Word? If so, it stands to reason that you cannot get victory over flesh problems.

As you meditate on this verse, ask God to help you become steadfast in your obedience to Him.

6. Then I would not be put to shame when I consider all your commands.

There is no shame in obedience to God, there is only shame in disobedience. A command is an uttered expression of a will (God's) which is to be obeyed. When God reveals His will to us, to obey it means we will have no shame when we stand before Him. What is the will of God? God's will in all things is to have mercy.

In Matthew 9:13 we read, "But go and learn what this means: 'I desire mercy, not sacrifice. . . .' " God desires mercy in all things. The will of God for every believer in every situation is to show mercy. If we would just obey that one command, we would never be brought to places of sacrifice. What are places of sacrifice? They are those places we bring ourselves to when we have been disobedient. The sacrifice is something we make or do after we have done wrong.

In 1 Samuel 15:22 we read, ". . . Does the Lord delight in burnt offerings and sacrifices as much as in obeying the voice of the Lord? . . ." To obey is better than sacrifice because obedience goes before sin, while sacrifice goes after sin. It's not that God does not accept our sacrifices and renewed commitments to Him. It is just that if we would simply obey Him in the first place we wouldn't be brought to the place where we need to make sacrifices.

Jesus said, "Go and learn what this means: I desire mercy." Mercy has been described as the ardent desire to meet the need of someone else. If we would go and do mercy to others, we would then learn that mercy is God's will for all people. If we would follow that single command, we would never be put to shame.

As you meditate on this verse, ask yourself if you show mercy to all people.

7. I will praise you with an upright heart as I learn your righteous laws.

An upright heart is a heart full of truth. ". . . The true worshippers will worship the Father in spirit and truth . . ." (John 4:23). The only way to enter into the true spirit of worship is through truth. We must have an upright heart to worship God. However, the upright heart is gained through learning what His righteous laws are.

Righteousness deals with our relationships with men, while godliness deals with our relationship with God. We are made righteous through the blood of Christ. However, being made righteous we are to go and do acts of righteousness. Righteous acts could be termed the right treatment of other men. It's treating men the way God has treated us. We cannot worship God with an upright heart if we have a wrong relationship with another man.

We who have the Spirit of Christ in us are to represent Him on earth. I do not represent Jesus if I hate another man. I cannot come to God and worship Him in the name of Jesus while I have something against another man. Mark 11:25 says, "And when you stand praying, if you hold anything against anyone, forgive him, so that your Father in heaven may forgive you your sins." If I have the sin of resentment in my heart, it is not an upright heart. I must have an upright heart in order to worship Him. I cannot gain the upright heart until I make everything right with my fellow man. I must do the same good to others that God has done to me.

Prayer plays a very important role in developing an upright heart. The more time we spend in the presence of God the more we see what God sees in others. The upright heart sees the things that God sees. Subsequently, those with this type of heart tend to treat others from that perspective.

As you meditate on this verse, ask God to help you develop an upright heart.

8. I will obey your decrees; do not utterly forsake me.

I will obey your decrees! That's a statement full of fortitude. "I will," is a strong statement in itself. "I will obey," is even stronger. What would give a person such resolve? Knowing that God will not forsake us gives us great resolve. We have a wonderful promise in the New Testament which says, ". . . Never will I leave you; never will I forsake you" (Heb. 13:5). The Greek meaning of the word "forsake" has to do with the way the soul abandons the body at the time of death. In other words, God's promise to us is that He will never abandon us; He will never take His life away from us.

A decree is a decision. David said that he would obey God's decrees (decisions). His obedience became his assurance that God would never leave him. When we follow God in His decisions we walk with Him. God rarely asks us to go do something for Him. He primarily asks us to go with Him. The work of God is not something we do on our own. It is something we do with God. When we walk in His decisions we walk with Him. God would never abandon those who walk with Him.

We live in a day where there is very little integrity. It is becoming more and more difficult to believe the mere promises of men. Fathers are abandoning their homes. Mothers are abandoning their children. Pastors are abandoning their flocks. Yet in the midst of it all, we have a promise we can cling to. "I will never leave you nor forsake you." "God is not a man, that he should lie, nor a son of man, that he should change his mind . . ." (Num. 23:19). Not only is God telling the truth, He also will never change His mind. What a comforting thought today.

As you meditate on this verse, focus in on that one thought. *I will never leave you nor forsake you!*

Beth

9. How can a young man keep his way pure? By living according to your word.

The word, "WORD" is a general term which includes, LAW, STATUTE, TESTIMONY, COMMANDMENT, PRECEPT, AND JUDGMENT. It refers to the utterances of God by which we live our lives. David, being a man, related best to men. However, this is applicable to all people, not just young men. The way we keep our lives pure is by submitting (bringing under) our "way" to God's Word. That Word may come through the Bible or through the spoken word. Regardless of how it comes, it is to be lived. It's when we "live" according to God's Word that our way remains pure.

When something is pure, it is not mixed with anything else. We are talking about a man's "way" in this verse. The only way for his "way" to remain pure is when his "way" is in harmony with God's Word. The Word of God, however it is received, is the only pure thing there is. All other "words" are mixed (not pure) with the motives of men. God's Word has only pure intentions. Men's words, no matter how godly they are, are all mixed with their own intentions.

This is a challenge to "come under" God. To live according to God's Word means we are to leave our ways, and bring ourselves under God. It means we must leave our way of doing things. It means we are to abandon our plans, goals, and ambitions. The impurity in our "way" comes from our self-centered motives. There is a life of purity available to all who will "come under" God. Our lives are full of impurity only when we come out from under God, or do our own thing and make our own decisions.

As you meditate on this verse, ask God to show you the impurity of your ways. Then ask Him to help you "come under" His ways.

10. I seek you with all my heart; do not let me stray from your commands.

A command (commandment) is an uttered expression of a will which is to be obeyed. When we seek God with all of our heart, the chances of us straying are minimized. However, we still have the ability to stray in the sense that seeking God does not remove our free will. The purpose of seeking God is to bring your will in line with His. When God has all of our heart, we won't want to stray, although we still possess the ability to do so.

Our heart is who we are. We have no existence other than what is in the heart. That's why Jesus said, "The good man brings good things out of the good stored up in his heart, and the evil man brings evil things out of the evil stored up in his heart. For out of the overflow of his heart his mouth speaks" (Luke 6:45). When we seek God with our whole heart, we are seeking Him with all that we are. David said that he sought God with his whole heart. That's convicting! Can you say the same? David is expressing his love for his God. "God, You have my whole heart, I keep nothing for myself; do not let me stray." What a powerful prayer!

The beauty of a relationship is that you have the freedom to walk away from it, but choose to stay with it. The beauty of my wife's relationship with me is that she has the ability to walk away from me at any time, but she wants to stay with me. If I were a master manipulator and so controlled my wife that she had no choice but to stay with me, even though she wanted to leave, where would the beauty be in that?

God will never violate our free will because He wants to know if we really want Him. When we willfully seek Him with our whole heart, we are giving ourselves over to Him. That gives us the desire to never stray from His commands.

As you meditate on this verse, ask God to show you the areas of your heart that you have not fully committed to Him.

11. I have hidden your word in my heart that I might not sin against you.

To hide the Word in our heart is to do more than just read the Bible or to memorize it. To memorize or read the Word puts it in our head. However, everything must get from the head to the heart before it transforms us. The heart is who we are. When we allow the Word of God to get deep within our heart, we are allowing it to shape the very essence of who we are.

The Word of God is hidden deep within the heart through the practice of prayer. God speaks to us in many different ways and at many different times. However, if we will take the Word that God speaks to us into the prayer closet, and talk to Him intimately concerning that Word, we will rise as new beings. In the secret place of prayer, the spoken Word of God becomes our sustenance. It becomes the very thing that gives us life and liberty. Prayer takes the Word of God and brings life to us. That new life becomes the very thing that keeps us from going back to the old way of sin.

Equally powerful is that of praying the written Word of God. When we pray the written Word of God, we express things we do not ordinarily express. Praying the Word of God teaches us to say the things the Holy Spirit wants us to say. The value of it is that it brings us into the knowledge of God while increasing our desire for God. This knowledge and desire keeps us from sin.

David said, "But his delight is in the law of the Lord, and on his law he meditates." God has always intended for His children to hide the Word in their hearts. Meditation accomplishes this in a most effective way. Meditation is done through running a particular verse over and over in your mind.

As you meditate on this verse, don't pray any words other than this particular verse.

12. Praise be to you, O Lord; teach me your decrees.

"Decrees" are decisions. In this case, they are the decisions God has made. In Psalm 63:4 we read, "I will praise you as long as I live, and in your name I will lift up my hands." The lifted hand is a sign of surrender or submission. With lifted hands we worship and praise our God. In essence the Psalmist is saying, "Through praise I learn Your decrees (decisions) because I am bringing myself under You." Bringing ourself "under" is what submission means. It means we are giving our will to God. We can now pray with Jesus, "Not my will but Thine."

Through submission, we gain a teachable spirit. Praise makes us teachable because of the submissive spirit we must be in, in order to worship God. The true worshipers not only worship in spirit but also in truth. We come into truth through being teachable. God does not force feed us. He waits for our spirit to open to Him so that He can gently teach us of himself. Matthew 15:8-9 says, "These people honor (worship) me with their lips, but their hearts are far from me. They worship me in vain. . . ." They worshiped God, but it was futile because their hearts were not pliable.

"The secret of the Lord is with them that fear him . . ." (Ps. 25:14;KJV). The secret of the Lord himself cannot be learned through study, but through submission. There is no way our limited minds can understand the Lord. A person's spirit must commune with His spirit. This is done through true worship of God. As we worship Him and lay our lives in His hands, we begin to understand things (decrees) about God that cannot be understood any other way. We learn more about God through submission than we do through self-exaltation. Pride is a lifting up of ourselves. Submission is a lifting up of God. When we bring ourselves down and worship from a position of lowliness He is exalted.

As you meditate on this verse, pray this prayer: "Father, bring me down."

13. With my lips I recount all the laws that come from your mouth.

The word "laws" has to do with the "teachings" of God. The Old and New Testaments are teachings on how to live. The Psalmist would recount all the things that God had taught him through the law. He recognized the source of his life as being his obedience to God. With his lips, he would declare all of God's laws. He knew that, "The law of the Lord is perfect, reviving the soul. The statutes of the Lord are trustworthy, making wise the simple. The precepts of the Lord are right, giving joy to the heart. The commands of the Lord are radiant, giving light to the eyes. The fear of the Lord is pure, enduring forever. The ordinances of the Lord are sure and altogether righteous" (Ps. 19:7-9).

David knew God's law to be his source of life. Therefore, he could declare with his lips the law of his God. He knew that the laws of God are "more precious than gold, than much pure gold; they are sweeter than honey, than honey from the comb" (Ps. 19:10).

David wanted to be kept from willful (presumptuous) sin (Ps. 19:13). He did not want to live a life of continually making sacrifices for his sins. He did not want to live a life of continually sinning on the premise that God would forgive him. He knew that obedience was better than sacrifice (1 Sam. 15:22). Therefore he wanted a clean heart. The heart is cleansed through meditating on and declaring the law of God.

"May the words of my mouth and the meditation of my heart be pleasing in your sight . . ." (Ps. 19:14). The words of our mouth and the meditation of our heart is pleasing to God WHEN it is centered on the Word of God. When our mouth is declaring His Word and when our heart is meditating on His Word, we are most pleasing to God.

As you meditate on this verse, ask God to make your words and meditations pleasing to Him.

14. I rejoice in following your statutes as one rejoices in great riches.

Statutes are distinctly laws laid down. They are explicit laws. The Psalmist would rejoice in these laws as one rejoices in great riches. Have you ever dreamt of great riches? The reason we think riches would be so wonderful is because we think it would mean we could live the kind of life we so desire. What kind of life do you really desire? Is it a life that finds its only fulfillment in material things? David understood that true wealth was obedience to God. He truly felt that following God's statutes would result in the kind of life that would give him true satisfaction. It was the kind of life that no material wealth could buy.

Our minds tend to get clouded by the spirit of this world. We see pictures of people winning millions of dollars in some type of contest, and they are depicted as the happiest people on earth. Their joy is understandable from a fleshly perspective. However, that which challenges us is David's rejoicing over the statutes of God in the same way a man rejoices over great riches. It takes a truly spiritual man to see that spiritual growth is as beneficial as temporal gain.

The Word of God teaches us that we are to take on the mind of Christ. Our carnal minds rejoice in getting all we can for ourselves. The mind of Christ says, "And if someone wants to sue you and take your tunic, let him have your cloak as well" (Matt. 5:40). If we struggle with the thought of giving someone our cloak, then we are fooling ourselves if we think we are as spiritual as David, who rejoices over the statutes of God.

As you meditate on this verse, ask yourself if you truly have the mind of Christ.

15. I meditate on your precepts and consider your ways.

No wonder God said David was a man after His own heart. David was absorbed with his God. He would meditate and consider the precepts of God.

"Instruction" is the term we generally use instead of precept. Has God ever instructed you in anything? Have you ever set aside time to simply meditate on that instruction? Have you ever considered His ways? I once worked for a large corporation. It was common to hear people respond to instructions with the phrase, "Who said I had to do that?" When the answer came, "The boss," there was no hesitation. We followed his instructions because we respected his position.

Without the daily practice of being in the presence of God and meditating on His Word to us, we tend to lose the reality of who God is. We don't lose our theological definition of God, we simply lose a real living sense of who He is. There is a great difference between the God we know in our head and the God we know in our heart. The head is full of rationale while the heart is full of emotion. The head takes a very legal look at God and bases its obedience on that. The heart takes a very loving look at God and bases obedience on that. The head cannot change the heart but the heart can change the head.

It's the heart that is changed through prayer and meditation. When we give ourself over to time in the presence of God, we are making ourself a living sacrifice. Through that, our heart begins to conform to the character of God. As the heart changes, the head follows suit. Eventually we are transformed by the renewing of the mind. Ultimately we take on the mind of Christ because we have taken Christ into the heart.

When we know God in the heart we tend to be more obedient to Him. We obey Him out of respect. His instructions become our meditation.

As you meditate on this verse, consider your level of respect for God.

16. I delight in your decrees; I will not neglect your word.

The Psalmist found his delight in God's decrees. Decrees are the decisions God has made. Have you ever asked God for directions and found that God actually gave them to you? When He directed you, did you delight in it or did you tolerate it? I have found many people following God's decrees, but hardly delighting in it.

Many times I have come upon a situation where I will say something like, "I see you are teaching Sunday school class." With quite a bit of disappointment in their voices they respond, "Yeah, God wants me to do it, so I have no choice, besides that, nobody else will do it. I'm just doing God's will." That may be following God's decree, but it is a far cry from delighting in it. The Psalmist's delight was to follow God's decrees and not neglect His Word.

In John 15:10-11 we read, "If you obey my commands, you will remain in my love, just as I have obeyed my Father's commands and remain in his love. I have told you this so that my joy may be in you and that your joy may be complete." Have you discovered the joy of obedience? Do you want to find a sad, frustrated person? Find one that God has given direction to, but who has remained disobedient. The joy of obedience is knowing that we have pleased God. That is why Jesus said that if we will obey, we will remain in His love. When we love God, our greatest desire is to please God. A number of times, during Jesus' earthly life, a voice came from heaven saying, "This is my beloved son in whom I am well pleased." The words I look forward to hearing more than any other are, "Well done, enter into the joy of the Lord." Our obedience to His decrees and Word will bring us to that place one day.

As you meditate on this verse, ask yourself if you truly delight in obedience to God.

Gimel

17. Do good to your servant, and I will live; I will obey your word.

Here David is asking God to do good to him so that he may live. All life comes from God, and because of that we are to live in obedience to His Word. God's Word, whether it is spoken or written, is the very source of our life.

To obey the Word of God is to do more than simply believe that it is the infallible Word of God. The word "obey" is a verb. Verbs demand action. To obey the Word of God means we must live what it says. That is the action that must follow belief. We cannot simply believe in prayer without having a prayer life. You may believe that there is such a thing called prayer, but to believe in it we must do it. The same is true of tithing; we cannot believe in it without doing it.

The goodness is in the doing, not just in the believing. We can believe all we want in prayer, but until we do pray, no good comes from it. To say with David, "Do good to your servant," we must be willing to do the Word of God. Life comes when we do (obey/practice) the Word of God.

Matthew 5:7 says, "Blessed are the merciful, for they will be shown mercy." Blessed are those who practice having mercy on others; through that, they receive mercy. This is one example of how the good that comes through obedience brings life. Mercy is life. Mercy is our salvation. God, through mercy, gave us grace. We are saved through grace. To continue to receive life (mercy) from God, we must have mercy on others.

As you meditate on this verse, ask God to show you areas where you can do His Word. Through this, He will bring life to you.

18. Open my eyes that I may see wonderful things in your law.

All that God teaches us through His law, statutes, testimonies, commandments, precepts, and judgments are life to us. However, our flesh tends to so cloud His life that we need a revelation to be able to "see." What we are talking about is spiritual sight, not physical sight. Paul once prayed, "I pray also that the eyes of your heart (understanding) may be enlightened in order that you may know . . ." (Eph. 1:18).

The question must be asked, "Does God give us wisdom apart from himself?" The answer is no! He cannot, for there is no wisdom apart from Him. First Corinthians 1:30 says, "It is because of him that you are in Christ Jesus, who has become for us *wisdom* from God — that is, our righteousness, holiness, and redemption" (emphasis mine).

Open my eyes that I may see wonderful things in Your law. To see Jesus is to see all things. Jesus is the fulfillment of the law. Jesus is the wonder of the law. God's law is not just a bunch of rules. His law is our means to life. All seeing (knowing) comes from God. There is no revelation apart from Him. It's from being in His presence that the eyes of our understanding are opened. His presence is His revelation.

From the beginning of time, God has been putting everything in order for the revealing of His Son. The entire Old Testament points to the coming Son of Man. In the Gospels, we have the account of when He came to earth the first time. The rest of the New Testament all points back to when He came. The Bible ends with the Revelation of Jesus Christ, the book which shows us the events surrounding His second coming. Everything in this entire universe points to the Son of God. To see Jesus is to see the wonder of God, it is to see the miracle of the law.

As you meditate on this verse, ask God to show you His "wonder."

19. I am a stranger on earth; do not hide your commands from me.

A command is an uttered expression of a will which is to be obeyed. The qualification for receiving or understanding His commands is that we be as strangers on earth. When we were separated from Christ, we were excluded from the covenants of the promise (Eph. 2:12). Now that we are one with Christ, we are strangers of/on this earth. We are to live an existence separate from this world's system. It's our separation that reveals God's commands to us. Separation from the world is the key to revelation.

Separation is the word used to describe both sanctification and holiness. Sanctification describes the process, while holiness describes the end result. In either case, they are both a separation. When we make ourselves strangers on earth, we are separating ourselves. This becomes the sum total of all revelation. How can God reveal anything about himself to those who are not separate from the world? However, the separation hurts! To understand healing, one must be separated from good health. In the midst of illness, God can "reveal" divine healing. It cannot be revealed any other way. The only way to understand God as a provider is to separate ourself from our money. When we give tithes and offerings, even though we cannot afford to, we "see" God as a provider. Living a separate life in this world enables God to reveal himself to us. The more the Church is like the world, the more clouded her revelation of Him becomes.

When we become strangers on earth, we become citizens of heaven. As citizens of heaven, we are to live an existence that differs from the rest of the world. We are to live our lives according to God's uttered will.

As you meditate on this verse, consider the "ways" of the world that may still be in you. Then determine before God, that you are going to become a stranger on earth.

20. My soul is consumed with longing for your laws at all times.

"For our God is a consuming fire" (Heb. 12:29). Our God consumes us. To give ourself to Him means we can no longer exist because God consumes us. When something is consumed, it is destroyed. David said his soul was consumed with a longing for God. The soul represents human nature. When the soul has been consumed with a longing for God, it has been destroyed of its humanness. Human nature is one of the primary obstacles to spirituality.

Galatians 5:17 describes this dilemma, "For the sinful nature desires what is contrary to the Spirit, and the Spirit what is contrary to the sinful nature. They are in conflict with each other, so that you do not do what you want." When the sinful nature is consumed or destroyed, we have wonderful spiritual freedom. However, the soul must be destroyed.

Everything that has physical life experiences hunger. The same is true of spiritual life. If we are spiritually alive, we have spiritual hunger. Spirituality is like carnality in this one sense: its craving is destined by its feeding. The more we feed it, the more it craves. If we were to respond to God each time we felt His prodding, soon we would feel His prodding more often. In time, our soul would be consumed (destroyed) with a longing for God.

David's soul was consumed with longing. This is where most of us differ from David. He was totally occupied with a longing for the Lord. There must be a longing in each of our lives if we are ever going to approach the spiritual craving of David's heart. David had a heart that chased after the heart of God. It has often been my prayer, "God give me a heart that wants You, a heart that longs for You, a heart that is completely taken up with You."

As you meditate on this verse, ask God for a heart that wants Him.

21. You rebuke the arrogant, who are cursed and who stray from your commands.

Arrogance, or the loss of humility, is the root of every sin and every evil. The reason they (the arrogant) are cursed is because they walk in conflict with the commands of God. All of the commands of God are expressions of His will which are to be obeyed. Obedience is the spirit of meekness. The meek person is willing to obey God in all things. Complete obedience to God will result in ridicule from other men. When a man is full of pride, he is not willing to take ridicule from other men. Thusly, he walks in disobedience to God so as to avoid the humbling experience of ridicule. When a man worships himself, he cannot handle ridicule because that tears at the very heart of what he worships. However, when a man worships God over himself, he can endure ridicule because he doesn't see himself as exalted. Subsequently, the meek do not stray from God's commands.

"The one who sows to please his sinful nature (arrogant), from that nature will reap destruction; the one who sows to please the Spirit (meek), from that Spirit will reap eternal life" (Gal. 6:8). The reason the arrogant are cursed is not because God has cursed them but because they are living in violation of divine order. The sinful nature simply reaps destruction.

Divine order is given for our protection. If it were not for the fact that God rebukes us when we are disobedient, we probably would never turn from certain sins. I was once talking to a man who had gone through a serious illness. He was telling me about how he was simply playing with his commitment to God. Finally, through his struggles, he committed his life deeply to God. He said, in reference to God, "Once Daddy spanked, I straightened out."

As you meditate on this verse, ask God to help you humble yourself in His presence.

22. Remove from me scorn and contempt, for I keep your statutes.

A statute is an explicit law. Jesus gave us a statute in the New Testament. In Luke 10:25 we read, "On one occasion an expert in the law stood up to test Jesus. 'Teacher,' he asked, 'what must I do to inherit eternal life?' " In verse 27, "He answered: 'Love the Lord your God with all your heart and with all your soul and with all your strength and with all your mind;' and 'Love your neighbor as yourself.' " If that statute is kept, scorn and contempt will be taken from you. Scorn and contempt cannot exist within the framework of love. If you truly love your neighbor the same way you love yourself, it will be virtually impossible to harbor negative feelings.

The key to this is not that in focusing on doing away with ill feelings, but in developing a heart that will keep God's statutes. We really have no choice in the matter. To remove scorn and contempt we must love.

"You have heard that it was said, 'Love your neighbor and hate your enemy.' But I tell you: Love your enemies and pray for those who persecute you" (Matt. 5:43). To remove scorn and contempt we must pray for our enemies. What happens when you pray for those who persecute you? You begin to love. What would happen if we prayed, "God, bless their (the enemies') lives. Shower them with fulfilling mercies. Bless their life the way You have blessed mine. Do the same good to them that You have done for me." Praying for them in this manner is called the mercy prayer. It will help us to fulfill the statutes, "Love your neighbor as yourself, and pray for your enemies," because it will cause you to see what God sees in them. When we pray for God to have mercy on someone else we begin to gain God's perspective.

As you meditate on this verse, ask God to show you areas where you still have scorn and contempt. Then remove them through praying the mercy prayer for them.

23. Though rulers sit together and slander me, your servant will meditate on your decrees.

A decree is a decision. It is a decision handed down to us by God himself. David knew that even though others were slandering him, his only option was to meditate and subsequently follow God's decrees (decisions).

David began his book (Psalms) by admonishing us to meditate on the Word of God. ". . . And on his law he meditates day and night" (Ps. 1:2). To meditate on the Word of God is to become absorbed with it. It is to give the mind over to it. Through that, we become as stable as a tree. "He [who meditates] is like a tree planted by streams of water . . ." (Ps. 1:3). Stability is a much needed quality for the one who feels that others are desirous of persecuting him.

David would meditate on God's decrees. Many times we feel quite justified in countering someone's slander of us in kind. However, God's decision on how to handle this is to turn the other cheek, it's to go the second mile, it's to pray for your enemies. If we would truly come to the revelation that vengeance is the Lord's, we would become as stable as a tree in the midst of persecution.

Bill Gothard once said, "Confidence is how little you react when falsely accused." When Jesus was brought before Pilate, He was falsely accused. However, He did not react. He was stable knowing first of all that vengeance is His Father's business, and that false accusations will ultimately be found out. In the midst of slander, meditate on God's decisions for your life.

As you meditate on this verse, ask yourself how you react to false accusations. If you would meditate on the Word of God, you would develop the stability of a tree.

24. Your statutes are my delight; they are my counselors.

The statutes of God were the Psalmist's delight! Are they yours? Do you find your delight in gaining your counsel from the explicit laws of God? A statute is a "law laid down," it is unswerving. If you are not flexible, an unswerving law will break you. I was once driving past a church that had a sign on their front lawn that said, "Blessed are the flexible, for they shall not be bent out of shape." The statutes of God are established, divine orders, that cannot be altered. The only way they could be our delight is when we desire to line up our life with God.

The captain of a ship was noticing the light of another ship approaching him one foggy night. He radioed ahead, "Change your course." The response came back. "You change your course." This made the captain angry for he knew he was the biggest ship in the immediate waters. A second time he radioed, "You are on our course, change your course." The response came back, "You change your course." Finally he identified himself and said, "This is the captain, change your course." The response came back, "This is the lighthouse, change your course."

Often we try to get God to line up with our lives and plans rather than lining up our lives with Him. We will say things like, "God, try to understand why I am the way I am." While we should be saying, "God, help me to become what You want me to be." We tend to think we are the center of life. We are not! The Word of God is the center of all things. Regardless of what we are going through, the Word of God stands true.

As you meditate on this verse, ask yourself if you can say with the Psalmist that the statutes of God console you.

Daleth

25. I am laid low in the dust;
preserve my life according to your word.

"The Lord God formed the man from the dust of the ground and breathed into his nostrils the breath of life, and the man became a living being" (Gen. 2:7). What an incredible thought — God formed us from dust, and then breathed His life into us. We came from dust, and we return to dust. Our only life comes from the One who created us. Isn't it interesting to think of how man rebels against God from time to time, thinking he can exist without the very One who gives him life. We have no existence outside of God; He is our very subsistence. To rebel against Him means certain death.

God breathed life into us. His breath, or Word, is the source of our life. God lives within His Word. His Word, the Bible, is our constant source of new life. The more we are in the Word, the more life we gain. We must be in the Word in order to be alive unto Christ.

It is not uncommon for us to use the phrase, "put to death." However, the phrase, "put to life," is not as familiar to us, though it should be. Have you ever prayed, "Put me to life according to Your Word," or "Put me to life through Your Word?"

David prayed, "preserve my life," which is what "put me to life" means. The name, "Jesus," means, "preserver." Satan is the destroyer. Jesus, the Word, preserves our life from Satan, the one who destroys life. In essence David's prayer goes something like, "I came from dust and I return to dust; I am nothing but dust. The only life I have comes from You; *life* me Lord, through Your Word."

As you meditate on this verse, pray for God to "*life*" you through His Word.

26. I recounted my ways and you answered me; teach me your decrees.

In essence David is saying, "I announced or declared my plans (ways) and God showed His approval of them by answering me." We are to never take pride in our own plan. We are to submit ourselves to the plan of God, and then line up our lives with it. Many people have great plans for God. They decide how He should answer prayers, they decide how He should heal, and how He should supply needs. It is very common to ask God to bless what we are doing, rather than to do what God is blessing. The blessings of God lie within His plans for us, not necessarily within our plans for Him. When our "ways" are the same as God's, He answers. I once saw a plaque that said, "If it pleases you to please God, you can go ahead and do as you please."

David then went on to ask God for further direction in understanding God's decrees. Decrees are basically the same as decisions. In this case, it would be God's decisions. When God sees that we want to be taught His decisions, He also sees that we have a desire to please Him. To desire to be taught His decisions is a sign of maturity. It's a recognition of our own inability to direct our lives without Him. "There is a way that seems right unto man but the end of it is death." We often think we know what is best for ourselves when in reality we don't. God does!

There is nothing more fulfilling than lining up our life with God's plan. God lives within His decisions. Psalm 16:11 says, "You have made known to me the path of life; you will fill me with joy in your presence, with eternal pleasures at your right hand." When we follow God's plan or path of life, we experience the fullness of joy.

As you meditate on this verse, ask yourself how desirous you are to be taught His decrees.

27. Let me understand the teaching of your precepts; then I will meditate on your wonders.

"Precepts" are instructions. David is asking for an understanding of the teaching of God's instructions. He wants to understand how God's instructions apply to life. There is no understanding outside of God. First Corinthians 1:30 says, "It is because of him that you are in Christ Jesus, who has become for us wisdom from God. . . ." Jesus is our wisdom from God. He is our understanding. To gain more understanding, we need more time in His presence. God is trying to convey His very life to us. His Word is not just an instruction book we are trying to learn. We are attempting to understand what the life of God is all about. How could it ever be learned outside of prayer? Through the door of prayer we enter into God's life.

Proverbs teaches us that if you spend time with an angry man, you will become angry; if you spend time with a wise man, you will become wise. We seem to take on the spirit of the people we spend time with. The same is true of God. The Fruit of the Spirit begins to develop within the heart of those who spend time in God's presence.

Through prayer we gain an understanding. That understanding is so incomprehensible, we simply stand in awe of our God. What we understand is, God is beyond our comprehension. Therefore our only option is to trust and obey His precepts. Our God is full of wonder. There are many things that are too wonderful to explain. For instance, I cannot explain how divine healing works, but I can testify to it. I cannot explain how God supplies our needs, but I can testify of it. Once David understood the teachings of God's precepts, he gave himself to meditating on God's wonders.

As you meditate on this verse, give thought to the wonders of God.

28. My soul is weary with sorrow; strengthen me according to your word.

David begins this section of Scripture (Daleth) by proclaiming he has been laid low in the dust. Then he expresses the weariness of his soul. It is not atypical for us to go through times of exhaustion. However, it's through the weariness, and times of exhaustion, that we realize our lives are beginning to accomplish something for God.

I once heard of a man who said, "We are not carnal beings having a spiritual experience, we are spiritual beings having a carnal experience." This is what Jesus expresses to us in Hebrews 10 :5, "Therefore, when Christ came into the world, he said: 'Sacrifice and offering you did not desire, but a body you prepared for me.' " Jesus was a spiritual being, who came from heaven, into a body that God had prepared for Him. God was not looking for sacrifices of animals and burnt offerings, although the law required them to be made (Heb. 10:8). That which God was looking for was someone who would willingly offer his own body in service to the will of God. "Then He (Jesus) said, 'Here I am . . . I have come to do your will, O God' " (Heb. 10:7). Jesus became the ultimate sacrifice because He offered His prepared body in service to God. When we do the same thing, it will result in weariness from time to time, it may even feel like total breakdown. However, it's because of what Jesus did through His body that you and I can experience salvation today. When we give our bodies for the doing of God's will, ultimately others will see Jesus and be saved.

We must learn, like David, to draw our strength through the Word of God. Remember our prayer, "put me to life"? It is applicable here also. "Bring new life or joy in me through Your Word."

As you meditate on this verse, thank God for the life that comes through His Word.

29. Keep me from deceitful ways; be gracious to me through your law.

Jesus is not only the way, the truth, and the life, He is also the only way into truth and life. Jesus is truth. The best way to be kept from deceitful ways is to go into Jesus. We need to become so absorbed with Him that we never want to come out into the flesh again.

David prayed, "Keep me from deceitful (lying) ways." The only reason for a lie to continue is to protect the liar from others discovering who he really is. Its source is pride. Pride is the basis for all deceit.

It is entirely possible that the only way to keep from deceitful ways is through the humbling of oneself. However, this humbling of ourselves becomes a problem if we fear how God will respond to us. We may even avoid humbling ourselves out of fear of what God may put us through. We forget too easily that, "God resists the proud but gives grace to the humble."

David then says, "Be gracious to me through your law." "Be gentle with me Lord." We are interesting creatures. When we are not very kind to God, we think He will respond to us in kind. God never responds to us according to what we deserve. He is full of grace and mercy. He gives grace to those who humble themselves.

The word "law" means "teach." Teach me graciously so that there are no deceitful ways in me. Jesus can teach us! In Matthew 11:29 we read, "Take my yoke upon you and learn from me, for I am gentle [gracious] and humble [no deceitfulness] in heart. . . ." We need never worry about what will happen to us when we humble ourselves, for God is gracious to us.

As you meditate on this verse, ask God to help you become more and more like the One who is humble and gracious.

30. I have chosen the way of truth; I have set my heart on your laws.

David has his heart set on the laws of God. Because of that, he has chosen the way of truth. We all have certain "ways" of doing things. We get dressed in a certain way, we eat our food in a certain way, we even drive our cars in a certain way. All of these "ways" have either been learned or chosen by us. When it comes to the law of God there is a "way" in which we are to live.

Whenever we are faced with temptation, a most important factor comes into play. At the point of temptation, we are faced with choosing a "way" in which to respond. Temptation puts our "way" of doing things to the test. It is a challenge to see whether or not we will follow God's way or ours. The "way" we choose determines the lordship of our life.

Have you ever considered how you concede to the lordship of Christ in your life? It's through our obedience to Him specifically during times of temptation. Temptation is a challenge to come out from under submission to God. David chose the "way" of truth, or God's way, because his heart was set on God's law. Not until a person's heart is "set" as David's was will he be able to constantly choose God's way during temptation. There must be an abiding love in the heart for something greater than oneself.

David's heart was set on God. He expresses it in Psalm 57:7, "My heart is steadfast, O God, my heart is steadfast. . . ." To be steadfast is to be fixed upon something in the same way one board would attach to another with a nail or screw. One board would be fixed to the other. When the heart is fixed or steadfast, there is no wavering.

As you meditate on this verse, consider the way of your life. Is it lined up with God's way?

31. I hold fast to your statutes, O Lord; do not let me be put to shame.

There is no shame in obedience to God. There is shame in disobedience to God. David is asking God to come to his defense only because he has been faithful to the statutes of God. God will always defend those who live in obedience to Him. Though there may be times of temporary setbacks because of our obedience, eventually there will be honor, not shame. If you are a person of conviction you will ultimately gain the respect of others even if they do not necessarily agree.

Mikhail Gusenberg, the man who brought the Communist message to China, was once asked why he put so much effort into his task. He responded, "I am not here for my health, or I would not be working in barbarous heat. I serve an ideology. And with an ideology, it is not numbers that count. It is dedication. It is not a matter of whether we enjoy our work here. The work is necessary. That is all that counts."[1] Gusenberg's ideology was wrong, however, his unswerving dedication to it is to be respected. He succeeded in bringing communism to China. He was sincerely wrong, but at least he was sincere.

As Christians we, too, should be committed to an ideology. Our ideology should be that of doing whatever is necessary to bring glory to our God. If that is our ultimate objective, then every subordinate decision should line up with that. Too often our objective is to get to heaven one day rather than to bring glory to God. Subsequently, we do not see service to God as something that should direct our lives. Therefore, any discomfort keeps us from working for Him.

It will take commitment to hold fast to the statutes of God the same way David did. David had a commitment to God that was driven by a deep love for God. We are to have nothing less than a heart that is just as committed to God as David's.

As you meditate on this verse, ask God for a deeper commitment to Him.

32. I run in the path of your commands for you have set my heart free.

In the previous verse we see David holding fast to the statutes of God. A man of strong convictions will ultimately experience some type of persecution in his life. Persecution is like a prison. When you are persecuted you feel separated from the rest of the world. If anyone understood this, David did. More than once David found himself imprisoned because of his convictions, although he was not literally in a prison. Because he would not violate God's statutes, he found his life being directed by those persecuting him.

David's convictions would not allow him to harm King Saul, even though Saul, while in pursuit of David, would have taken his life. Because he honored God, his life became subject to the whims of others. However, David discovered the secret of being set free in the midst of his prison. He learned that God can enlarge a heart (set it free). David had the freedom to run in obedience because God had enlarged his heart.

As a father, I never take any pleasure in seeing my son suffer; but when he does, I draw near to him in a special way. When he was little, he was afraid of the dark. When he went to bed he would crawl under the covers and hide. His bed became a prison to him. If I happened to enter his room, suddenly he had all sorts of freedom. He was free to get out of bed and actually look under his bed or go into his scary closet. My presence set his heart free. He could literally run throughout his room. This is how God sets our hearts free! If, through obedience to God, we have come into some type of prison or persecution, God draws near to us in a way that we cannot experience through any other means. This sets us free in the midst of our prison. His presence has enlarged our hearts in the midst of our persecution. We are then able to literally run in obedience to Him.

As you meditate on this verse, consider the freedom there is when God sets your heart free.

He

33. Teach me, O Lord, to follow your decrees; then I will keep them to the end.

Teach me to follow. That's a statement of love. David says in essence, "Lord I want to follow You forever." He didn't intend to follow God temporarily or when it was convenient. He intended to follow Him to the end, or right up until the day of the Lord's return. Jesus teaches us that this type of commitment will be equally important to us, especially in the last days.

In Luke 18:8 it says, ". . . When the Son of Man comes, will he find faith on the earth?" By the time Jesus returns, will He find those who have followed Him up until the very last days? The Bible indicates that in the last days, times will be difficult. Men's hearts will fail them for fear of what is coming on earth. There will be a growing apostasy in the Church. In the parable preceding Jesus's words, He teaches us of the need to persist in prayer. It begins by saying, "Then Jesus told his disciples a parable to show them that they should always pray and not give up" (Luke 18:1). This expresses David's heart when he said, "I will keep them (decrees) to the end."

David's key was that he was a follower of God. He said, "Teach me to follow." Many of us want to be leaders rather than followers. We say, "Teach me to lead." We study leadership, we read about great leaders, and we are fascinated with champions. The problem is that we cannot be leaders of men until we are followers of God. David was content with God getting all the glory. Subsequently, he could follow God even when things were not going so well. When the Son of Man returns will He find faith in your heart? He will if you are a follower of God.

As you meditate on this verse, consider whether you are content with following, or must you lead?

34. Give me understanding, and I will keep your law and obey it with all my heart.

The greatest understanding we can attain is knowing that we can trust God even though we cannot fully understand Him. This is why Proverbs 3:5 says, "Trust in the Lord with all your heart and lean not on your own understanding." We must realize there is a vast difference between our understanding and God's. When we consider the incomprehensible qualities of God, including His unfailing love, we begin to realize that God understands from a perspective we simply do not have, and will never have.

Mrs. Albert Einstein was once asked to explain her husband's "Theory of Relativity." After pondering the question for a moment she stated, "I cannot explain his theory at all, but I know Albert, and he can be trusted." In a similar way, the parent-child relationship requires the same development of trust over time. There are times when a parent will ask a young child to simply obey them. The child may reply, "I don't understand why I should obey." The parent responds with, "You don't need to understand, you just need to obey!" There are some things parents cannot explain to their children and children cannot understand because they lack the experience and maturity of the parent. However, if a child will simply trust and obey, it will work to his benefit. The songwriter had it right when he wrote, "Trust and obey, for there's no other way to be happy in Jesus, but to trust and obey."

As you meditate on this verse, consider whether you trust God's understanding and simply obey, or whether you require Him to first explain according to your understanding before you obey.

35. Direct me in the path of your commands, for there I find delight.

There is a path of delight for those who follow God's commandments. In Proverbs 22:6 we read, "Train a child in the way he should go, and when he is old he will not turn from it." "Training" means more than just taking our children to church and teaching them about God. There is certainly nothing wrong with teaching our children about God. Training a child in the way he should go has very little to do with church attendance. However, when we train someone, we teach them by doing, in their presence, what we want them to do. In other words, we live the life we want them to live.

David wanted to be directed in God's path. God has a path, or that which comes naturally, for each of us. Proverbs goes on to tell us in chapter 30:18-19, "There are three things that are too amazing for me, four that I do not understand: the way of an eagle in the sky, the way of a snake on a rock, the way of a ship on the high seas, and the way of a man with a maiden." There is a naturalness in each of these cases that is hard to explain. It is an expression of the inborn desire or drive that God has put in each of us. We experience delight when we are following in the path God has designed for us. If parents can find the intrinsic path God has for their children and train them in it, the children will have a life full of delight.

"There is a way that seems right to a man; but in the end it leads to death" (Prov. 14:12). Man's way is death, God's way is life. When we line our lives up with the commands of God, we discover the natural path God has for us. Therein we find the fullness of delight.

As you meditate on this verse, ask God to show you the natural path He has designed for you.

36. Turn my heart toward your statutes and not toward selfish gain.

This is possibly the most powerful prayer in this entire Psalm. Turn my heart toward You, and not toward me! Herein lies the battle of the ages, "My will or God's; my gain or God's!" The benefits of serving God are so tremendous that one could serve God for selfish gain. Ezekiel encountered this problem, "My people come to you, as they usually do, and sit before you to listen to your words, but they do not put them into practice. With their mouths they express devotion, but their hearts are greedy for unjust gain" (Ezek. 33:31). Ezekiel was telling the Israelites that although they were verbalizing their praises, they were not truly worshipping God. Their hearts were greedy for unjust gain.

Why do we seek God? Do we seek God so we can use God, to fulfill our ends, or do we seek God so God can use us to fulfill His ends? There is a world of difference between these two motives. Think of the error there is in seeking to gain from the One who gave His life for us. Jesus came to earth to empty himself for you and me. To take advantage of what serving God means is error. The Christian is subject to many blessings. He works hard, he is honest, and he is loyal. These qualities alone will bring blessings. To use those blessings for personal gain is a mistake. There is one reason for gain. It is so we can continue to meet the needs of others. David asked for his heart to be turned from greed to God.

This life is not about selfish gain, it is about selfless devotion. The church of Laodicea focused on selfish gain. It had the nicest building in town, the sharpest people in town, and the latest programs available. It was rich, it had need of nothing. It had everything but Jesus. Jesus says in Revelation 3:20, "Here I am! I stand at the door and knock. If anyone hears my voice and opens the door, I will come in. . . ." Jesus was on the outside trying to get in.

As you meditate on this verse, pray the essence of David's prayer: "Turn my heart from gain to God."

37. Turn my eyes away from worthless things; preserve my life according to your word.

Worthless things are vain, or, empty things — things that exalt self over God and have no eternal value. Worthless things are dead things. They have no life in them, therefore, they bring no life. The only life we have is from God. That is why David ends his thoughts by saying once again, "Preserve my life." *Life* me! To pray, "preserve my life according to Your Word," would be like praying, "*Life* me as I focus on Jesus, Your Word."

The key to this is in turning our eyes from self to God. David further emphasizes some of his thinking from verse 36 where he prayed, "Turn my heart from gain to God." In that verse he was dealing with the heart. In this verse he is dealing with the eyes.

The eyes are what actually fill the heart. Our heart is who we are, and we are what our eyes have allowed into our heart. "The eye is the lamp of the body. If your eyes are good, your whole body will be full of light. But if your eyes are bad, your whole body will be full of darkness . . ." (Matt. 6:22-23). The good eye, or the single eye, is an eye that only sees Jesus, or only sees what Jesus sees. It does not focus on self or vanity. It is an eye that is not turned inward; it sees beyond itself to others and their needs. If your eyes are good, your whole body will be full of light, or Jesus. If your body is full of light, there is no room for darkness. That's what Jesus meant in saying that the only way for the body to be full of darkness is through eyes that are bad. The bad eye focuses on self. It looks upon everything in an attempt to see how self can benefit. Focusing on ourselves opens the gate for all evil. Whenever our needs and desires become more important to us than the desires and needs of others, we fill ourselves with darkness.

As you meditate on this verse, pray David's prayer, "Turn my eyes away from worthless things, turn them toward You."

38. Fulfill your promise to your servant, so that you may be feared.

We inherently have a desire for God to be God and we glory in His glory. The most devastating thing we could discover would be to find out that God was not able to fulfill His Word.

As a young boy I had great hope in my earthly father. It was not uncommon to hear us on the playground boasting about our dads. "My dad is stronger than your dad," or "My dad is the best carpenter in town." Whether or not dad was strong or weak, short or tall, handsome or not, was not the issue. The issue was whether he was faithful or not. Did he live up to his word? Did he fulfill his promises? These are significant concerns of all little children. We tend to have ideals and expectations of our parents that may be difficult, if not impossible, for them to live up to. However, as children we long for those things to be true of them. We want them to be the best. My father used to be one of the world's strongest men, but that was because I was only four years old at the time. When you are four years old, your father is one of the world's strongest men, also (at least to you).

David was expressing that type of feeling when he said, "Fulfill your promise. . . ." In other words he was saying, "Be all that You say You are, God, because all my hope is in Your faithfulness to Your Word." We could easily pray along with David, "Be the Lord of lords and the King of kings, for then my reverence for You will be strengthened. Then I will fear You as I should."

It is good practice to periodically express to the Lord all the things you believe He is, listing His attributes and qualities. This will serve as a reminder of your constant need to revere your God.

As you meditate on this verse, think about who God really is.

39. Take away the disgrace I dread, for your laws are good.

The things which we probably dread above all others are our failures before God. We dread our disobediences to Him, for such things are a disgrace to us. They hang over us like a black cloud. However, God can remove the disgrace.

The word "laws" in this verse means "teachings." God's law is our teaching. If we follow His laws, He will remove the disgrace of our past by bringing us into judgment. Nevertheless, His judgments are good for they are designed to separate good from evil in our lives.

Another term for laws could be, "customs." In some cultures, customs are so strict and ingrained into the society that to break one could mean death. However, when a person opens himself to God and begins to follow His laws, a dividing takes place in his life. This dividing between two opposing ways of doing things judges one as "right," and the other as "wrong." God's judgments are meant to maintain His true customs and are designed to remove the evil and leave the good.

I once heard a saying that has become a favorite of mine: "God saved me, not only knowing what I was, but He saved me, knowing what I would become." It is not uncommon for believers to feel they have failed God and to be filled with disgrace. Sometimes they may even think, *God is probably upset with the fact that He even saved me in the first place, since I have failed Him so much.* Nothing could be less true! God not only knew what you were, He also knew what you would become, and yet He saved you. There is obviously something God knows about you that you do not know about yourself.

As you meditate on this verse, thank God for removing your disgrace, then ask Him to help you submit more and more to His laws.

40. How I long for your precepts! Preserve my life in your righteousness.

David longed for the precepts of God. "Precepts" denotes what we generally mean by "instructions." In any position of responsibility, explicit instructions are given for doing whatever is a person's charge. In our position as believers we are instructed to treat others righteously. Righteousness deals with our relationship with others. Godliness deals with our relationship with God. To treat someone in a righteous manner would be to treat him the way God treats us.

David was mistreated many different times in his life. King Saul pursued him in an attempt to kill him. This caused David to live on the run for some time. Later in his life his son Absalom rebelled against him in an attempt to take his kingdom from him. Absalom even attempted to kill his own father. However, when David heard of his son's death he cried out, ". . . O my son Absalom! My son, my son Absalom! If only I had died instead of you . . . (2 Sam. 18:33). Love like that comes only from the heart of Jesus.

David longed for righteousness. Jesus emphasized in the New Testament, "Blessed are those who hunger and thirst for righteousness, for they will be filled" (Matt. 5:6). David hungered and thirsted for others to be treated properly. When that is our longing also, we too will be filled with God's righteousness. Whatever we long for we will eventually be filled with, whether good or evil.

David ends his prayer with, "Preserve my life in your righteousness." In whatever way we treat others, we will be treated. "So in everything, do to others what you would have them do to you . . ." (Matt. 7:12). David longed for others to be treated righteously. Therefore, his life was preserved because of the righteousness of God. God treated David the way David treated others.

As you meditate on this verse, consider whether or not you long to follow God's precepts.

Waw

41. May your unfailing love come to me, O Lord, your salvation according to your promise.

The cry of David's heart is for the unfailing love of God. He is longing for the Messiah. Jesus is the unfailing love of God. Throughout all of the Old Testament, we see the prophets and patriarchs looking for the first coming of their Messiah. Today, after His birth, death, and resurrection, we continue to look for Him but with a different focus. We still look for the unfailing love of God but we also look for His second coming. We have our salvation through His blood. Now we long for His return.

Have you ever considered why you long for Him? It seems so often that we seek His return so He can take us away from the drudgery of this world. If that is our only motive, we miss the greater blessing of longing for Him. David longed for the Messiah himself. It will certainly be a wonderful experience to enter into His presence. However, there is another facet to this we should consider. It is that of being a blessing to Him.

Martha Wing Robinson once said, "He did not ask for you to have experiences: it was not that we should be wonderful. He asked for yourself for one purpose, that He might have you for himself."[2] It seems that we are always looking for some wonderful experience in our walk with God, and when we run into peril we ask Jesus to come and take us out of it. That really is not longing for Him, or even taking Him into consideration. That is more of a focus on self. Have you ever considered what it would be for you to be Jesus' wonderful experience?

As you meditate on this verse, contemplate on that great day when Jesus returns, and takes you up in His arms like a child. On that day, you will be His wonderful experience.

42. Then I will answer the one who taunts me, for I trust in your word.

This is a continuation of the previous verse. David is looking for the promise of God so that he can answer those who are taunting him. This is not an unfamiliar situation for believers to face. It is common for Jesus to be mocked and for Christians to be ridiculed. In that sense, we too look for Him. We look forward to the day when every knee will bow and every tongue will confess that Jesus is Lord! That will be the day when all our efforts to serve Him will come to fruition, when all of our consecration to His Word will be worth it all.

Our answer to those who taunt us, needs to be Jesus himself. However, this is not to be presented in a vengeful way. We should not long for the Son of God to be revealed simply for the purpose of telling someone else, "I told you so."

When I first surrendered my heart to Jesus, many of my friends taunted me for that decision. I didn't want them to see who Jesus really is just to prove myself right. These were my friends! I cared for them. My honest desire was for them to see Jesus, not only so they would stop taunting me, but rather that they themselves would surrender their lives to Christ.

It should always be our desire that Jesus would be as merciful to others as He is to us. In that light, we should never desire vengeance for anyone. "Look, he is coming with the clouds, and every eye will see him, even those who pierced him; and all the peoples of the earth will mourn because of him . . ."(Rev. 1:7). When Jesus is revealed to a lost world, we will not need to add a single word. His manifestation will say it all. They will see that they are lost when they see Him. Our desire should be to bring as many into Christ before that day as we can.

As you meditate on this verse, ask God for a heart of mercy rather than a heart of vengeance.

43. Do not snatch the word of truth from my mouth, for I have put my hope in your laws.

This verse is dealing with hypocrisy. David is saying that anyone who fails to walk his talk does not deserve to be a steward of the truth of God's Word. He said, "I have put my hope in Your laws." David so believed that God's Word was true that he patterned his life according to it. He maintained the customs (laws) of God. Thus when he spoke, his words were true. The Pharisees on the other hand, had the word of truth snatched from them because they did not walk their talk. They were hypocrites. They may have spoken the Word of God but there was no life-transforming truth in their words because they broke the commands of God for the sake of their traditions (Matt. 15:3).

God's Word proves to be true when it actually shows forth as evidence in a life. If a man preaches that God can deliver another while he is in need of deliverance himself, his words lack truth and persuasiveness. Proverbs 16:23 says, "A wise man's heart guides his mouth, and his lips promote instruction." That is what David did not want taken from him. He wanted the word of truth (persuasiveness) to remain, and to assure that it would, David patterned his life after the laws of God.

Are your words true? Do you tell people to do things that you haven't done? Do you tell people to stop doing the very things you are still doing? God never offers solution without sacrifice. In other words, God never asks us to do anything that He hasn't done himself. When Jesus tells us to turn from sin, it is because He turned from sin. When He tells us to love our enemies, it is because He loves His enemies. When He tells us to turn the other cheek, it is because He turns the other cheek. The reason Christ's words are so powerful and persuasive is because He speaks the word of truth from His heart.

As you meditate on this verse, ask God to give you, "the word of truth."

44. *I will always obey your law, for ever and ever.*

This is a simple statement of David's love for God. "I will obey you forever." David considered his commitment to God as something without end. He understood obedience to God to be forever. It doesn't end at the time of death; it goes on into infinity. We are prone to make commitments only for a specified period of time. It is very typical for us to discipline ourselves up to a certain point. We go on two-week diets, or twelve-month exercise programs. Most of our commitments have a time limit. However, when we consider our obedience to God, we need a different frame of mind.

Everything about this earth has a beginning and an end; therefore, it is natural for us to think in those terms. Yet, when it comes to God, we need a heavenly frame of mind. God has no beginning and no end. Heaven is a permanent state. The popular hymn says, "When we've been there ten thousand years." The problem with that is, we won't be thinking in those terms once we are in heaven. Consider what the Bible says regarding time and heaven: "But do not forget this one thing, dear friends: With the Lord a day is like a thousand years, and a thousand years are like a day" (2 Pet. 3:8). At best, 10,000 years will only seem like 10 days. When we get to heaven it will seem as if only moments have passed by for those loved ones who went before us.

It would be to our own benefit to start thinking with a heavenly frame of mind rather than an earthly one. We have surrendered our hearts to Jesus, for forever, not just for now. Our commitment to His Word is everlasting, for His Word says, "Heaven and earth will pass away, but my words will never pass away" (Luke 21:33). There is no time frame in heaven, there is only eternity. David had a heart of commitment forever. He loved God more than he loved himself. Subsequently, his commitment was everlasting.

As you meditate on this verse, ask yourself how heavenly minded you are.

45. I will walk about in freedom, for I have sought out your precepts.

David sought out the precepts of God. "Precepts" means "instructions." The precepts (instructions) of God are given as to what to do, when to do, how to do, etc. David discovered the freedom of obedience in patterning his life after the precepts of God. Typically, we consider instructions as perimeters or boundaries. We sense a loss of freedom when we must follow them. Our sense of loss actually contradicts God's intent in giving us His precepts.

John 8:36 says, "So if the Son sets you free, you will be free indeed." Only freedom comes in the form of forgiveness. Jesus forgives. The only freedom there is, is in forgiveness. When we are forgiven we are free of self worship. Self worship is sin. To forgive someone puts them on the same level as you. If you worship self you want to keep yourself above them. "Jesus replied, 'I tell you the truth, everyone who sins is a slave to sin'" (John 8:34). It is interesting how people in the world think they are free because they do not obey the precepts of God. Yet in truth, they are in bondage to the worship of self.

David said, "I walk about in freedom." Freedom only comes through obedience to God. The one who walks in obedience is free to have his life inspected. He needs to cover nothing. Is your life an open book? Would you feel free to have anybody inspect your walk?

If there is an area of sin in our life, we walk about in secret. If we have not sought out and submitted to the precepts of God, we walk in bondage. People who feel "free" from any sense of obedience to God, are actually slaves to the sin that controls their lives.

As you meditate on this verse, consider whether you actually seek to know God's instructions for your life, or if you do your own thing.

46. I will speak of your statutes before kings and will not be put to shame.

Have you ever done any name dropping? Why do we do that? Is it to gain some type of status? It is very convenient for us to use someone of stature to gain access, acceptance, or even credibility. In our world, we work hard to become acquainted with those of influence. If we can say we know someone, it speaks well of us, especially in a society that worships men over God.

When we speak of the statutes of God, it is different than when we speak of knowing men. When we testify of knowing Jesus, we can't take any credit for it. Knowing Jesus comes through surrendering ourself to Him. No one can take any self glory in that. The kingdom of God is for those who are poor in spirit, those who keep giving themselves away. It is a humbling thing to realize that we cannot gain God through our own efforts. In the world's eyes Christians are often viewed as weaklings. They are viewed as not being strong enough to be their own people because they have given their lives to Jesus. Instead of asserting themselves they have given themselves away.

David knew something the world does not know. He knew there was no shame in speaking about the things of God. David knew the one true King. He knew that his King would not put him to shame. David saw things in light of eternity, while we are prone to only see things in light of today. If we were to stand before an earthly king, would we be awe-struck, or would we have the perspective David had? David knew he was talking to mere men who were earthly kings, about the King of kings. There was no shame in that. Even if the world presently does not respect our King, one day they will. One day they, too, will bow and worship Him.

As you meditate on this verse, consider whether you speak boldly about your King or whether you still speak of Him rather timidly.

47. For I delight in your commands because I love them.

This is a continuation of the previous verse. The reason David saw no shame in speaking of the things of God, even to earthly kings, was because he loved the commands of God. There is no shame in loving God. When we love something, we submit to it. Submission requires that we bring ourselves under the authority of the one to whom we have submitted. In that light, our only life comes through our obedience to that one.

Obedience should always be the result of submission. When we simply are obedient to someone, we tolerate their rules. However, when we submit to someone, our obedience is coupled with a desire to obey. The basis for such submission is love, and that love compels us to obey. Obedience to God based solely on what one should do, without a desire to obey, may in essence mean there is no submission at all.

David said that his delight was in the commands of God because he loved them. Through his obedience, he found life. Jesus said, ". . . I have come that they may have life, and have it to the full" (John 10:10). To be full of life, we must be full of the kind of obedience that comes from submission.

God is found in the obedience of men. To enter into the presence of God, we must submit to Him. There is more to following God's commands than simply doing them. In our desire to do them, we find the life of God. In Ephesians 4 we are instructed to put off our old corrupted self; to put away lying, and to speak truth; to no longer steal, but to labor; to no longer allow corrupt communication to rule our tongue, but that which is good. In so doing, we will not grieve the Holy Spirit (Eph. 4:22-30). Just as the Holy Spirit is grieved by our disobedience, His presence is enhanced by our obedience.

As you meditate on this verse, ask yourself if you truly love the commands of God.

48. I lift up my hands to your commands, which I love, and I meditate on your decrees.

David lifted his hands to God. The lifted hand is symbolic of surrender or submission. If someone put a gun in your back, by lifting up your hands you indicate you have surrendered to them. David stated that his life was surrendered to God. What is it to surrender to someone? It means we become their captive. They own us. We are subject to their whims. To become captive to mere man could be quite devastating. However, you always dwell in places of safety when you are a captive of God.

David was a bondservant of God. A bondservant places himself in a position wherein the Lord has complete mastery over him. A bondservant is one who has the freedom of choice but chooses to continue to serve out of love. In Luke 2:29 we read of Simeon who said, "Sovereign Lord, as you have promised, you now dismiss your servant in peace." The word Lord in this verse is not the typical word for Lord. It literally means authoritarian or dictator. Simeon looked upon himself as the servant of the Lord under His absolute mastery. The Lord was his complete master. Simeon was a mastered, subdued, and subjugated man.

To think of the Lord as a dictator becomes negative only when we do not want to be controlled. David loved his God. He did not view being a bondservant as a negative thing because his desire was to be controlled by God. He submitted himself to God. He lifted his hands in surrender to his God. This was what separated David from most others. Today we don't often understand such devotion. We tend to live for ourselves and to use God to get our way. We don't see Him as the One who has complete mastery over us, yet we are quick to call Him Lord. Luke 6:46 says, "Why do you call me, 'Lord, Lord,' and do not do what I say?"

As you meditate on this verse, consider the Lordship of Jesus in your own life.

Zayin

49. Remember your word to your servant, for you have given me hope.

Hebrews 1:1 tells us that God spoke to the prophets in many different ways. God has the ability to speak to us through others, through prayer, through a prophetic voice, or even through a miraculous sign. However, the most common way for God to speak to us is through His Word, whether written or spoken.

Have you ever had the Word of God speak to you? Has God ever given you a Scripture in a time of need that you have desperately clung to? David expressed that very thing. He is saying in essence, "My hope is in your Word, please don't forget your promise to me."

In David's lifetime he had many experiences. He single-handedly killed a lion. He felled Goliath with a stone. He was pursued by King Saul who was trying to kill him. He was a mighty warrior. Toward the end of his life things changed for him. He fell into sin with Bathsheba and he had her husband murdered. Throughout all his many trials David's standard was the Word of God.

The Word of God is the only standard of truth this world can ever know. It is the only thing upon which we can base our entire future. It is not only an accurate record of the past, but of the future also. There are many times when the only hope we have is in what God says in His Word about the future.

The Word of God is our hope. Just as David said, "For you have given me hope," we must also say the same. If we fail to put our hope in His Word, we will have no hope. Men's hearts are one day going to fail them out of a fear of what is coming on earth (Luke 21:26). However, those who know the Word of God have a stability this world cannot understand.

As you meditate on this verse, contemplate the role the Word of God plays in your own life. Is it your hope?

50. My comfort in my suffering is this: Your promise preserves my life.

Once again, David is expressing trust in the Word of God. The only comfort he knows during his time of suffering is found in the Word of God. However, he found more than simple comfort. He states that the promise (God's Word) preserved or quickened his life. The Word of God put him to life, which is the opposite of being put to death.

There is more to life than simply breathing and having good health, things that have to do with our physical life, though they are important to our earthly existence. David's emphasis was more than just these things. He stated, "Though I may be suffering in my physical condition, I find comfort in it." The comfort he found was the very life of God himself. In essence he said, "Your promise brings the very life of God to me."

Matthew 5:4 says, "Blessed are those who mourn, for they shall be comforted." God draws near to those who suffer in a very special way. When we are suffering in body, we tend to take the Word of God more seriously. We tend, in those times, to read it with great interest and cling to every promise we read. In our needy state, we find that our very life comes through the Word of God.

All life comes from God, and God lives within His Word. The prophet Isaiah expressed it this way, "But those who hope in [wait upon] the Lord will renew their strength. They will soar on wings like eagles; they will run and not grow weary, they will walk and not be faint" (Isa. 40:31). This is a promise that actually preserves our life.

As you meditate on this verse, ask God to "LIFE YOU" though His Word.

51. The arrogant mock me without restraint, but I do not turn from your law.

In this verse, we see one of the primary battles of the ages: the proud against the humble. When David says he will not turn from God's laws, he is expressing his willingness to obey God. Willingness to obey necessitates a spirit of meekness. Only the meek can truly obey God in the face of mockery. It is commonplace to perceive meekness as weakness. Not so! In actuality it takes tremendous strength to stand in opposition to one's peers.

Meekness portrays strength of character. The arrogant lack character. Subsequently, they cannot restrain their mockery for others. Arrogant people are full of pride or self. They attempt to exalt themselves by demeaning others. They do not possess the kind of character qualities required to show restraint. David clung to the law of God even though he was being challenged to break it. He expressed humility. The humble (meek) are willing to endure because their obedience to God is a primary motivator in their lives. This kind of humility was displayed by Jesus when He stood before Pilate. The arrogant mocked Him without restraint, yet Jesus did not retaliate in the way they expected He would. Instead, He obeyed the law of His Father. Jesus knew that His obedience to His Father was far more important than their false accusations about Him. Instead of coming to His own defense, He turned the other cheek and died for them.

Mockery and persecution are a testing ground to prove if we are as meek as we think ourselves to be. It is one thing to consider oneself humble when we are not facing any kind of criticism, but it is an entirely different thing to actually put humility into practice in the face of arrogance.

As you meditate on this verse, consider how you react when falsely accused.

52. I remember your ancient laws, O Lord, and I find comfort in them.

The word "laws" in this verse is translated "judgments" or "customs." Judgments are the decisions by which a custom is established. It's like saying, "These are the laws of the land." The judgments of God are the decisions He has made in order to establish the customs, or way of life, for the people of God.

David found comfort in God's ancient laws. Even today, if the ancient laws of God, or the Ten Commandments, were the standard by which we lived, we, too, would be comforted. The Ten Commandments are basic to the health of any society. When men live in obedience to these laws, they live in relative comfort. For instance, one of the Ten Commandments is "You shall not murder." If everyone followed that law, society would not be in the state of anxiety it finds itself today.

Another ancient law of God is, "You shall not steal." A friend of mine had an occasion to visit Japan with a group of people. A girl from their party accidentally left her purse on a bench in a public park. Hours later they returned and found the purse still there. The custom in Japan, even today, is that you do not take what is not yours. What comfort there would be if only men lived in accordance with God's ancient laws.

David purposely remembered, or called to remembrance, the ancient laws of God. We would do well to do the same. When was the last time you purposely set aside time to dwell on the Ten Commandments?

As you meditate on this verse, consider God's ancient laws. You shall have no other gods before Me; you shall not make for yourself an idol; you shall not misuse the name of the Lord your God; remember the Sabbath day by keeping it holy; honor your father and your mother; you shall not murder; you shall not commit adultery; you shall not steal; you shall not give false testimony against your neighbor; and you shall not covet.

53. Indignation grips me because of the wicked, who have forsaken your law.

In this verse David is continuing his thoughts about the laws of God. In the previous verse, he expressed the comfort he found in obedience. Now, in this verse, he voices indignation toward disobedience. Righteous indignation! The word "righteous" indicates the right or godly treatment of others. Righteous indignation signifies a type of constructive anger, being upset for the right reasons. In contrast, our tendency is to simply get angry at people and call it righteous indignation. Oftentimes our anger (indignation) has nothing to do with righteousness.

What is it that upsets us when our own children disobey? Do we want to destroy them because of their disobedience? Do we pray, "God, annihilate my children because they forsake your laws?" Never! Yet we seem to pray that way for others. We forget God has no desire to destroy those who disobey Him. His intent, to bring them to obedience, is founded in a love which is even greater than the love we have for our own children.

When our children disobey us become upset because of the damage it brings to their lives. We want them to obey for their own good. More importantly, we want them to obey, so that God can be glorified through them. If our indignation is truly centered around the glory of God, then it will not be directed toward the disobedient person himself. It will be more focused on the spirit of disobedience which has gripped the heart of that man. Ephesians 2:2 says that the prince of the power of the air (Satan) is the spirit that works in the children of disobedience. Our indignation should be directed toward that spirit more than toward man.

As you meditate on this verse, ask yourself if you direct anger towards others or towards the spirit of disobedience.

54. Your decrees are the theme of my song wherever I lodge.

Do you have a song in your heart? Do you find yourself going throughout your life, much less your day, with the praises of God on your lips? God's decrees were the theme of David's song wherever he lodged. David had a great heritage to draw from. As God's children were wandering through the wilderness they would sing of Him. As they journeyed to Zion for special religious holidays they would sing of Him. "Great is the Lord, and most worthy of praise . . ." was one of their songs (Ps. 48:1). As they travelled they looked for the holy mountain where Zion was located. When they were close enough to actually see the city they would sing, "It is beautiful in its loftiness, it is the joy of the whole earth . . ." (Ps. 48:2). What a sight it must have been to see thousands of God's people walking to the city of God to worship Him. Wherever they lodged for the night their praises could be heard echoing throughout the stillness of the night. "Great is the Lord, and greatly to be praised in the city of our God, in the mountain of his holiness. Beautiful for situation, the joy of the whole earth, is Mount Zion on the sides of the north, the city of the great King (Ps. 48:1-2;KJV).

Today we are not much different than the people of old. We, too, are looking for the city of God. When we get a glimpse of our future it should cause us to sing. The songwriter has it right in his classic, "Amazing Grace:" "When we've been there ten thousand years, bright shining as the sun, we've no less days to sing God's praise, than when we first begun." Our song of praise will never end. Revelation 15:3 tells us about a day yet to come, "and sang the song of Moses the servant of God and the song of the Lamb: 'Great and marvelous are your deeds, Lord God Almighty. Just and true are your ways, King of the ages.' " One day all of heaven will sing out this song and those left on the earth will listen with envy as our praises fill the universe with worship of our King.

As you meditate on this verse, ask yourself if you have a song in your heart.

55. In the night I remember your name, O Lord, and I will keep your law.

"In the night I remember your name." There is a stillness in the night that creates a wonderful setting for intimacy with God. God instructs us in His Word to be still and know that He is God. Daytime represents activity. Typically it is during the day that we are most active. When God calls us to be still, He may be calling us to a place of intimacy with Him. There is something about stillness that brings us close to God. When we cease from our own activities, we develop a greater understanding that He is God. Many times in our "doing" we forget that God is ultimately in control. Our "doing" becomes our god. Could it be that God is calling you to cease from your own labor and simply be still?

Night can also refer to a dark time. Often we pass through "dark times" in our lives. This could be a phase that lasts for some time. David had many dark times in his life but he never gave up on God. He said that in the night he would remember the name of his Lord. The only one who can bring us out of darkness is He who is the Light of the World. The one who is Wonderful, Counselor, Mighty God, Everlasting Father, and Prince of Peace is the one who brings the light of day to our darkness.

David also said that even though he was in the "night" he would still keep God's laws. This quality is what distinguishes David from most of us. Our tendency is to use the dark times as an excuse to disobey God. We feel that our situation is exceptional and therefore God will understand our lack of obedience to Him. David said in essence, "Even though I can't see the light of day, I will still obey your laws."

As you meditate on this verse, consider how often you call upon His name in the stillness of the night.

56. This has been my practice: I obey your precepts.

This verse expresses the testimony of all spiritual men. There are two parts to David's testimony. The first is: "This has been my practice." This statement reveals a consistency in David's life that obviously enhanced his relationship with God. Consistency gives strength to all things. In order to develop spiritual strength, there must be a practice or a consistency in spiritual activities. Consistency must be evident in our pursuit of God.

We are not called upon everyday to put our physical strength to the test. However, as a result of consistent exercise, we develop a source of extra strength we can draw from in a time of need. The same is true spiritually. Our faith may not be put to the test everyday, but if we pray daily, we will have a source to draw from when we need extra faith.

The second part of this testimony is, "I obey." Obedience is the pinnacle of wisdom. There is no application of wisdom without obedience. Wisdom alone does not benefit man. Throughout the Book of Proverbs, we find that wisdom is always connected to obedience. In essence it says, "the wise man obeys." Who could be "wiser" than the one who is completely obedient to God in all things.

All through the Word of God we see those who obeyed God as the ones who were able to bless and minister to Him. In Ezekiel 44 we read about the priests, the descendants of Zadok. These priests continued to obey God when the other priests went astray. In verse 16 we read of the descendents of Zadok, "They alone are to enter my sanctuary; they alone are to come near my table to minister before me. . . ." To consistently obey is the ultimate way to bless God.

As you meditate on this verse, ask God to make you one of those whose life is a blessing to Him.

Heth

57. You are my portion, O Lord; I have promised to obey your words.

David said that God was his portion or life. In Exodus 16:4 God states, ". . . I will rain down bread from heaven for you. The people are to go out each day and gather enough for that day. In this way I will test them and see whether they will follow my instructions." When God sent the manna for His people, He asked them to gather just enough for each day. He sent them a portion large enough to sustain life. They were not to gather enough manna for two days in a row (except for the sixth day) because it would spoil. Each day they would receive bread from heaven in just the right portion for their need.

In John 6:35 Jesus said, "I am the bread of life. . . ." Jesus is the bread of heaven. Consider what Jesus was praying in the Lord's prayer when He said, "Give us today our daily bread." He is teaching us of our daily need of Him. We need "daily" bread. What we gained of Jesus yesterday through prayer is not sufficient for today. Yesterday's spirituality will grow stale and rot today.

David ended this verse by saying, "I have promised to obey." It takes strength to obey God. Manna provides that strength. Our daily portion of Jesus is what enables us to live in obedience to God. However, obedience drains us, for it requires that we give away, or empty ourselves. Through continued obedience, a natural hunger and need for refilling occurs within us as we persist in giving up ourself. Without obedience there would be no hunger or sense of need, for we would remain filled with self. In Numbers 11:6, the Israelites typified this fullness of self which comes through disobedience, as they complained, "We never see anything but this manna." They were literally tired of Jesus, the Bread of heaven.

As you meditate on this verse, pray this prayer; "Lord, You are my portion, give me today my daily need of You."

58. I have sought your face with all my heart; be gracious to me according to your promise.

In the Song of Solomon 4:9 we read of the groom's words concerning the bride, "You have stolen my heart, my sister, my bride; you have stolen my heart with one glance of your eyes. . . ." With a single glance of our eyes, we can make the heart of God flutter. David understood the intimacy of his relationship with God, thus he says, "I have sought your face." One of my favorite illustrations is that of the two types of seekers found in the Scriptures: seekers who are beggars and seekers who are lovers.

Seekers who are beggars look to the hand. On many occasions I have been approached by beggars. They are interested in one thing; what will my hand pull out of my pocket to give to them? Thus they look to the hand.

Seekers who are lovers look to the eyes. When someone is in love, the most important thing to them is to know that the one they love, loves them in return. Subsequently, they look to the eyes because the eyes tell the story. The Old Testament often encourages those who love God to seek His face, and yet we often only seek His hand.

It is not uncommon to read God's declaration, "My arm is not shortened." In other words He is saying, "I can reach you where you are; don't worry about My hand. I will be there to meet your needs, seek My face."

David sought the face of God with all his heart. His words in Psalm 27:8 express his innermost feelings, "My heart says of you, 'Seek his face!' Your face, Lord, I will seek."

As you meditate on this verse, ask yourself if you seek His hand or His face.

59. I have considered my ways and have turned my steps to your statutes.

David considered his ways. To be able to even consider our ways requires us to examine the freedom of our will. It is from this same freedom to choose our way that we may or may not choose to even consider our way. Much of the Christian walk constrains us to reshaping our will. Too often it is our will versus God's will. Yet a man can exercise his will over God's. He can, in the sense that Christianity does not demand that we give up our free will. Being a Christian means our will should be submitted to God's but you can choose not to do so.

If God were to take away our free will, He would remove the whole essence of what a relationship means. The beauty of a relationship is the free will. If I were able to manipulate my wife's life so that she had no choice but to live with me, what fulfillment would there be in that? The beauty of my wife's relationship with me is that she has the freedom to leave, but wants to stay with me. Similarly, God could manipulate us, but He is not interested in making puppets out of His people. He wants those who want Him.

David considered his ways and then he turned. Turning obligates one to repentance. David repented of placing his will over God's. I can easily relate to David here. Many years ago, I also considered the way of my life and realized that it was not God's way. I was following the way of man's reasoning. Scripture teaches us that there is a way that seems right to a man, but the end thereof is death. I was on that path of death because I had lived my whole life placing my will over God's. So I turned my steps toward His statutes (repented) and gave my life to Him.

As you meditate on this verse, consider the "way" of your life. Does it line up with God's way?

60. I will hasten and not delay to obey your commands.

In the previous verse David turned his steps toward the statutes of God. In this verse, he is running (hastening) toward God. Life is very fleeting. The reality of life's transient state will never be more real than when we stand before the Lord one day and realize how much time we wasted on things of little intimacy with Him. David hastened to obey! We should do no less.

In the Song of Solomon 1:4 we read, "Take me away with you — let us hurry! Let the king bring me into his chambers. . . ." The bride, in this verse, is expressing her craving to be brought into intimacy with the groom. "Take me away with you," is a simple prayer which expresses a longing for God and God alone. The "chamber" is literally the bedroom. The bride understands the urgency of being brought into this place of closeness with God, so she says, "Let us hurry!"

To pray this simple prayer of "Take me away with you," will eventually move us into intimacy with God. This prayer helps us to overcome all of the fleeting urges of life so that God alone is our true desire. Did you know that Jesus does not want to be number one on your list? HE WANTS TO BE YOUR ENTIRE LIST! Jesus is not interested in being one of many loves. He is not even interested in being the one we love more than our other loves. He wants to be the only love of our life. When He is our only love, our prayer life will reach a new level of intimacy with Him.

A person hastens to obey God only when there are no hindrances in his relationship with Him. Every hindrance to obedience reveals the existence of other loves in our life.

As you meditate on this verse, pray the simple prayer, "Take me away with You."

61. Though the wicked bind me with ropes, I will not forget your law.

David feels bound by the evil of men in this verse. The wickedness of the ungodly often threatens our freedom. However, David has found the freedom of obedience to God. In the midst of persecution, he declares, "I will not forget your law." In the New Testament, Jesus sums up the law with these words, " 'Love the Lord your God with all your heart and with all your soul and with all your mind.' . . . And the second [commandment] is like it: 'Love your neighbor as yourself.' All the Law and the Prophets hang on these two commandments" (Matt. 22:37,39-40). David knew he had to keep this law even though he was being mistreated.

What does the cross of Calvary mean to us? Obviously it serves as a re-minder that Jesus died for us. However, there is another meaning to it also. The Cross means the righteous die for the unrighteous. It means the godly die for the ungodly. To take up your cross and bear it means that you are to give your life for the sake of others. David was doing just that in this verse. Though the wicked bound (persecuted) him with ropes, he did not forget God's greater law of dying for the sake of others.

Jesus taught us that confidence is how little you react when falsely accused. When He was before Pilate, he didn't even defend himself because He knew that the accusations were false. He knew that truth would eventually win out. David practiced this also when King Saul sought to kill him. He certainly would have been justified in defending himself. Instead he allowed vengeance to be God's role, not his.

As you meditate on this verse, consider your reaction to those who falsely accuse you.

62. At midnight I rise to give you thanks for your righteous laws.

David would rise to give thanks. Thanksgiving is one of the most spiritual acts we can involve ourselves in because it is the only thing we can actually offer God. We have nothing to offer God other than this one simple thing. It was David who taught us to "enter his gates with thanksgiving and his courts with praise; give thanks to him and praise his name." It's humbling to be able to do nothing more than thank God for His goodness to us. We naturally would like to do something "significant." In God's eyes, thanksgiving is most significant. The kingdom of God comes to those who ask for it, not to those who try to earn it. Having done nothing to earn it, all we can do is humble ourselves and give thanks for it.

David would rise from his sleep to give thanks. Sleeping is one of the more carnal things we do. Nothing nurtures the flesh like sleeping. However, sleeping is not an evil activity because God created each of us with a basic need for it. Not only is giving thanks a spiritual activity, but to deny yourself of one of your fundamental needs in order to give thanks reveals a little of David's heart.

We often think of midnight as the middle of the night. Actually it is the beginning of a new day. David had a heart that wanted to put God before everything. At the beginning of each new day, David would rise to thank God for His righteous laws.

When I was courting my wife-to-be, I willingly missed some sleep just to be with her? Why? Because I wanted to be with her. If I could have arranged to meet her each night at midnight, I would have done that also. Just as we each have these same desires, we should also have a longing to be with God.

As you meditate on this verse, ask God to give you a heart of thanksgiving; a heart that longs for God.

63. I am a friend to all who fear you, to all who follow your precepts

David considered himself a friend to all who feared God. Not only are we automatic friends with those who fear God, we are family, also. If we fear God and follow His precepts, it's because we are part of His family. The word "precept" is what we generally refer to as "instruction." To be in the family of God, we follow God's instructions to us.

In Matthew 12:47, someone told Jesus that His mother and brother were outside. Jesus then asked the question, "Who is my mother, and who are my brothers?" In verse 50 He answers His own question, "For whoever does the will of my Father in heaven is my brother and sister and mother." There is one constant in the will of God. It is God's will, in every case, for the Son of God to be revealed through the kindnesses we do for others. In all that we do, it is the Lord's will for others to see Jesus. They see Him through the mercy we have on them.

David said he was a friend to all those who revered (feared) God to the point that they followed God's instructions. Jesus said that those who are in His family are the ones who do the will of God (follow His instructions). Jesus was not being unkind to His earthly mother when He was told that she was outside and He responded with, "Who is my mother?" He was not excluding her at all. He was simply revealing to us that we, too, can be in His family. We do not earn membership in the family of God through good works. However, if we are a true member of the family of God, it will be revealed by our kindness to others.

As you meditate on this verse, consider whether you respect God to the point where you reveal Jesus in all your actions.

64. The earth is filled with your love, O Lord; teach me your decrees.

David is asking to be taught the decrees of God. A decree is a decision. In this case, they are decisions God has made. Obviously God decided to reveal His love through His creation. The whole earth is filled with God's love. Nevertheless, it is quite apparent that our world is suffering from the effects of the fall of man. What this verse reassures us of is all things good and lovely are from the Lord, even in this fallen world. It is actually the love of God that keeps this world from completely destroying itself.

Love is the balance to all the evil in this earth. For every evil act, there is to be a countering act of love or mercy. It may be that evil things get more attention in this world. Yet, in actuality, good things far outnumber evil things.

The earth is filled with God's love, and because of it, we gain an understanding about God's decrees. It teaches us that even in an evil world, God's will is for us to be merciful to others. God's decision (decree) is to continue to have mercy on others, even on an undeserving people. Mercy is what will keep them from completely destroying themselves before God has an opportunity to lead them to repentance. Our own decision should be that of following this decree. We are to be living a life of returning good for evil. When we show kindness to others, the world begins to see that the earth IS filled with His love. They begin to see that the source of kindness is Jesus. Let the fact that the earth is full of the mercy of God get deep into your heart so it will motivate you to be part of this revelation to others.

As you meditate on this verse, ask God to give you a heart of mercy.

Teth

65. Do good to your servant according to your word, O Lord.

God does good to His servants! Are you a servant, or do you like to be served? If you have the spirit of Christ in you, you should have a desire to serve others. Jesus came not to be ministered unto but to minister. We are attempting to gain the mind of Christ through meditating on these verses. What becomes quite obvious as we meditate on them is that being served gives much more pleasure to our flesh than serving does. When we think we really are something, we want to be served rather than to serve.

Paul tell us in Philippians to have the mind of Christ. Then he gives us a description of Christ's mind as he says that Jesus ". . . made himself nothing, taking the very nature of a servant . . ." (Phil. 2:7). The servant's nature is that of nothingness. A servant is to be a conduit. He is to be the source of blessings for others. I once heard a minister say these words: "What makes a conduit or pipe effective? Nothingness! A pipe must have nothing inside of it in order for it to do what it's designed to do. When a pipe is filled with itself, it no longer can serve others."

To some, being nothing is a frightening thought. They say things such as, "How will our needs be met if all we do is serve others?" The answer to that is, the goodness of God is given to those who serve. God does good to His servants. What could be missing in a life where God is bringing good into it? If we look to be served by man, then all we have to look forward to is what man can bring into our life. If we look to serve others, then we can look forward to what God will bring into our life.

As you meditate on this verse, ask God to show you how you can become more of a servant. Let that mind be in you.

66. Teach me knowledge and good judgment, for I believe in your commands.

Knowledge and good judgment define the word "wisdom," in a much truer way than does the word "intellect." Many times intellectualism and wisdom are miles apart. The Bible tells us that the fool says in his heart there is no God. No matter how intelligent a person is, if he says there is no God, he is a fool and he lacks wisdom. James 1:5 tells us that we can pray for wisdom, "If any of you lacks wisdom, he should ask God. . . ." The wisdom given by God is all the knowledge and understanding needed to live a consistent Christian life.

Wisdom is knowledge and good judgment. A study on the subject of wisdom in the Book of Proverbs would show that it consistently connects wisdom to obedience or good judgment. In essence what it teaches us is that the wise man obeys God. He uses the knowledge God has given him to make good judgments. The pinnacle of wisdom is obedience to God. It would be virtually impossible to cite an example of a man wiser than one who is completely obedient to God. There is no greater wisdom than that.

Wisdom is found in David's words, "I believe in your commands." A command is an uttered expression of a (God's) will which is to be obeyed. The interesting thing about wisdom is that it comes through obedience, and obedience then produces more wisdom. The more we obey the commands of God, the more we do things the way God wants them done. With time and experience we begin to take on the mind of Christ. This results in more wisdom, more knowledge, and good judgment.

As you meditate on this verse, give some thought to the things God has taught you through obedience.

67. Before I was afflicted I went astray, but now I obey your word.

David is revealing something very important in this verse. It's a revelation of how we develop obedience to God through tribulation. Jacob, a great example of this, began life as a supplanter and a deceiver. Jacob would trip people up. However, one day he came face to face with his God. In Genesis 32 we are told how he wrestled with an angel of the Lord all night long. By daybreak, he was a different man. As a result of this encounter with God, Jacob walked with a limp the rest of his life because the angel of the Lord touched his hip. Even his name was changed. He became known as Israel.

Before Jacob was afflicted he went astray, but now he obeyed. God touched him in the hip to constantly remind him of his need for Him. Jacob used to trip people up. If the hip socket is weak, one can hardly even walk on it much less use it to trip others. God weakened Jacob so that His (God's) strength could be perfected in him. That weakness would be his constant reminder of how much he was dependent upon God.

The story is told of a shepherd who had a little lamb that constantly strayed away from the herd into dangerous areas. In order to teach the lamb obedience, the shepherd broke one of his legs. The shepherd then carried the lamb around his neck until the leg healed. During the healing process, the lamb's affection for the shepherd grew to a point that once he was able to walk on his own, he never strayed again. He may have walked with a limp, but he never strayed again. In this same way, our afflictions can actually serve as a protection, keeping us from truly harmful things.

As you meditate on this verse, consider the afflictions of your life and thank God for His protecting hand on you.

68. You are good, and what you do is good; teach me your decrees.

David is continuing his thought from the previous verse. Even though God may allow affliction in our lives, we must always remember that God is good, and what He does is good. Affliction is a type of judgment. Judgment is the separation of good from evil. We may view affliction as being anything but good. However, if affliction brings us to a place of learning His decrees, it is ultimately good for us. A decree is a decision God has made. To view all of God's decisions in light of His goodness helps us to accept them. All that God does, He does for our good.

Hebrews 5:8 says, "Although he was a son, he learned obedience from what he suffered." Even the Son of God learned through affliction. What if Jesus had not learned obedience and then disobeyed His Father? That would have been the greatest tragedy man would ever have known. Jesus knew that God is good, and even suffering is ultimately for good.

Hebrews 12:5-6 sheds more light on this, ". . . My son, do not make light of the Lord's discipline, and do not lose heart when he rebukes you, because the Lord disciplines those he loves. . . ." To be able to express God's goodness in the face of affliction is a sign of maturity. It's accepting the disciplines of life as a part of God loving us and shaping us.

In Psalm 103:10 we read, "He does not treat us as our sins deserve or repay us according to our iniquities." We must always remember, the goodness of God is not expressed in what we are going through. It is expressed in how He has kept us from going through all we deserve. We deserve eternal punishment. We deserve an eternity separate from the presence of God. The next time you suffer affliction, thank God for keeping you from all you deserve.

As you meditate on this verse, thank Him for His goodness.

69. Though the arrogant have smeared me with lies, I keep your precepts with all my heart.

The word "precept" generally means "instruction." "Instructions for living" can be expressed as "precepts." As children of God, we have been given instructions through the Word of God as to how we should conduct our lives. Jesus, the living Word, is our supreme example. When He was smeared with lies before Pilot, His response was to not react at all. He knew His Heavenly Father would ultimately take care of things and that vengeance was the Lord's, not His.

Jesus did, however, respond to their smears. He prayed, "Father, forgive them, for they do not know what they are doing" (Luke 23:34). Jesus prayed for forgiveness of those who smeared Him. Long before He ever went to the cross, He taught us to pray for our enemies. In Matthew 5:43-44 we read, "You have heard that it was said, 'Love your neighbor and hate your enemy.' But I tell you: Love your enemies and pray for those who persecute you."

Pray for our enemies! That's a tough precept to follow when we feel we have been smeared. The great lesson here, though difficult to learn, is that life does not revolve around us. God is the center of life, and obedience to Him is our highest call. The biggest problem we have with following God's precepts is in the humility it takes to follow them when we feel our rights have been violated. Not until our hearts want what God wants will we be able to follow Him at all times.

David said, "I keep your precepts with all my heart." In essence he was saying, "Your precepts describe who I am," because the heart of a man is who he really is. If you want to see into the heart of David, look at the precepts of God. David was a man who prayed for his enemies. David was a man who meditated on the Word of God, a man full of mercy. God's precepts detail David's life.

As you meditate on this verse, ask God to help you in your obedience to Him.

70. Their hearts are callous and unfeeling, but I delight in your law.

The callous and unfeeling heart is a reference to the "arrogant" in the previous verse. David kept the precepts of God with all his heart. The arrogant one's heart has a single focus — self. David's heart delighted in the law of God. He delighted in putting God first. The arrogant do not like the message of self-denial because that would ruin all that they are trying to accomplish in life. Those who are arrogant in their knowledge of God find no difficulty in stepping on others, even brothers and sisters in Christ. Their hearts have become callous. Somehow they have come to believe that what they are doing pleases God because they are getting the job done.

Jesus had the perfect balance for being both task-oriented and people-oriented. Jesus set His face like a flint concerning His purpose. Nothing could sway Him from accomplishing what God wanted Him to accomplish. However, in the midst of that, He never lost sight of the needs of those around Him. The fact is, there will never be anything that God calls us to do that doesn't focus on the needs of others. The task before us, the call of God on every Christian's life, is to do the will of God. What is God's will in every situation, the will of God for every Christian? It is to have mercy on others. There is no will of God outside of this one thing.

The arrogant chafe at the thought of having mercy on everyone because that might hinder them from accomplishing their goals. The humble see all others as better than themselves, subsequently they love the law of God. They love to show mercy to others because it exalts Christ. The arrogant want to exalt themselves.

As you meditate on this verse, ask God to show you the calloused areas of your heart, areas that are more concerned with your accomplishments than the people around you.

71. It was good for me to be afflicted so that I might learn your decrees.

Can you say along with David that affliction is a good thing? David said it was good because it caused him to learn more things about God. We tend to believe that our comfort is more important than anything else. When you stand before God, what is it that will give you peace of mind; the comfort you lived in, or your obedience to God? We must come to the realization that nothing is more important than obedience to God.

First Timothy 1:19 says, "Holding on to faith and a good [clear] conscience. Some have rejected these and so have shipwrecked their faith." If I have learned anything about the prayer life, it's the clear conscience one develops from it. Many times prayer is simply hard work. I don't always feel God in my prayer time. I don't always have the sensation that my prayers are even being answered. However, the one thing I always feel is the satisfaction a clear conscience gives me.

Consistency in our obedience and in our pursuit of God is what gives us a clear conscience. Without a clear conscience, we shipwreck our faith. Without faith, we cannot please God (Heb. 11:6). When we stand before God, our obedience to Him is what will give us peace of mind.

Not until we see the great need for, and benefit of, obedience to God will we ever have a proper perspective on affliction. The apostle Paul wrote about the fellowship of Christ's sufferings. He said that the intimate knowledge of Christ gained through suffering was worth more than all the gold in the world. He said everything outside of fellowship with God is worthless. There is no life outside of God. Therefore, fellowship with Him is the essence of life. If affliction brings us into greater intimacy with God, then it is a good thing.

As you meditate on this verse, ask God to help you know that fellowship with Him is more important than your comfort.

72. The law from your mouth is more precious to me than thousands of pieces of silver and gold.

The law from your mouth, or the spoken word; is there anything sweeter than that? There are very few instances in the Bible that have more significance than when God actually spoke to someone. Hearing the spoken Word of God will change any man's life. Saul of Tarsus was a well-educated man, circumcised on the eighth day, from the tribe of Benjamin, a Hebrew of the Hebrews, a Pharisee and Zealot. However, on the road to Damascus, he saw a light and heard these words, ". . . I am Jesus, whom you are persecuting. . . . Now get up and go into the city, and you will be told what you must do" (Acts 9:5-6). Those spoken words changed his life forever. Those very words continued to motivate him for the rest of his life.

David said, "The law from your mouth is more precious . . . than gold." What would you prefer? Would you prefer an unlimited supply of silver and gold, or access to the presence and words of God? Most of us prove, by our actions, that we prefer silver and gold over God. Our jobs can make tremendous demands on us and yet we sacrifice to keep them. They can take us away from our families for long periods of time. They even keep us from sleep. Our pursuit of silver and gold mandates our lifestyle while Jesus cannot get us to attend church with any regularity. If only we felt like David, that the things of God are more precious than money.

Living in obedience to His law is what sharpens our spiritual hearing. Not until we love that which proceeds from His mouth more than we love this world, will we develop David's kind of obedience to Him. That obedience brings us into a communion with Him. That obedience generates His presence.

As you meditate on this verse, express to the Lord your desire to follow His law.

Yodh

73. *Your hands made me and formed me;*
give me understanding to learn your commands.

David reveals something very crucial to life in this verse. God made us and formed us! He is the potter, we are the clay. In designing us, He created a place within us for Him to dwell. His dwelling place is to be in our hearts. The heart defines who we really are. The heart's condition determines how much spiritual understanding we have. When our heart is conditioned toward God, our ability to understand His commands increases. When our hearts are surrendered to God, then God becomes our life.

Psalm 49:3 says, ". . . The utterance from my heart will give understanding." There is no understanding outside of God. David asked God to give him understanding so that he could learn His commands. That understanding came through the utterance of his own heart and the still small voice of God.

A.B. Simpson once asked, "Is there any note of music in all the chorus as mighty as the emphatic pause? Is there anything that can so touch our hearts as the power of stillness?" There must be a stillness in our lives if we are to gain understanding from God. God waits in the depths of our being to talk to us — if we would only get still enough to hear His voice. Getting still is not just a matter of being quiet. It's more a matter of removing the ever-present sounds of self and pride from the heart.

In Psalm 46:10 we read, "Be still and know that I am God. . . ." The emphasis of this verse is that we need to stop all of our own efforts to do things and simply let God do them. The problem we encounter lies in our desire for self-glory. We like to be able to say, "I did it!" David's understanding came from knowing that God made him and formed him, and that he was to simply be still.

As you meditate on this verse, ask God to help you be still.

74. May those who fear you rejoice when they see me, for I have put my hope in your word.

God lives within His Word. To put our hope in His Word is synonymous with putting our hope in God. Romans 4:18 says, "Against all hope, Abraham in hope believed and so became the father of many nations. . . ." Have you ever put your hope in God against all odds, fully expecting God to honor your faith, and then find that everything seemed to go all wrong? If so, you are not alone. God will ultimately award you for your faith, but some things take time. In those times of waiting for God to act, we need to have our hope in His Word.

The Word proves itself true in the lives of those who fear God. David was a testimony to that. He said, "May those who fear you rejoice when they see me." In essence he was saying, "May those who see the faithfulness of God in my life rejoice, knowing that the same demonstration of mercy can be in their lives also."

We have all heard the phrase, "Do as I say, not as I do." Paul the Apostle, like David, said, "Do as I do." That's a powerful statement. In Philippians 4:9 we read, "Whatever you have learned or received or heard from me, or seen in me — put it into practice. And the God of peace will be with you." Would you find it comfortable or uncomfortable to say to another, "Do as I do, and you will be drawn close to God?" Can those who fear God rejoice when they see you, knowing that their hope in the Word will one day pay off for them regardless of what they are currently facing?

As you meditate on this verse, ask God to help you be an example others can follow.

75. I know, O Lord, that your laws are righteous, and in faithfulness you have afflicted me.

God's laws are righteous. What does righteousness mean? Righteousness has to do with our relationship with men, while godliness has to do with our relationship with God. We are made righteous through the shed blood of Christ and no other way. We cannot earn righteousness, however, being made righteous, we are to do acts of righteousness. Revelation 19:8 talks about the righteous acts of the saints, which make up her wedding garment. Acts of righteousness have to do with the right treatment of other people. Anything I do for another in the name of Jesus is an act of righteousness.

David said, God's laws are designed for our right treatment. Subsequently, God allows affliction when necessary. When we violate the righteous laws of God, we will ultimately experience affliction. To treat others cruelly or to seek vengeance is to be in violation of the righteous laws of God. Therefore, because of the righteousness of God, He must allow affliction in our lives. Affliction may be the most merciful thing God could do to us because of how affliction brings us back to God.

We have a choice in the matter. We either live a life of obedience or we live a life of sacrifice. Because of affliction, we are brought to places of sacrifice. First Samuel 15:22 says, ". . . To obey is better than sacrifice. . . ." The reason obedience is better than sacrifice is that obedience goes before sin and sacrifice comes after sin. If we will obey, we will not sin. If we sin, the righteousness of God will allow affliction, which brings sacrifice and renews fellowship with God. Once we commit our life to Him, He begins a work in us which He is going to continue right up until the day Jesus returns. He loves us too much to not bring us back into obedience.

As you meditate on this verse, thank God for His faithful afflictions and that He never gave up on you, even when you gave up on Him.

76. May your unfailing love be my comfort, according to your promise to your servant.

Since the time of Jesus, there has not been a greater example of love than that expressed through the heart of a mother. Jesus is obviously the greatest earthly example of love we have ever seen, but a loving mom certainly typifies that love. Mothers display unfailing love for their children that comes straight from the heart of God.

A story is told of a rebellious son who, in an act of violence and hatred, took a knife and cut out the heart of his own mother. In a panic he began to run from the scene with his own mother's heart in his hand. When his foot struck a large rock, he stumbled and fell to the ground. As he struggled back to his feet he heard his mother's heart say, "I hope you didn't hurt yourself, my son."

How many times have we cut out the very heart of God through our own disobedience to Him, and yet found that His greater concern was for our well-being? How many times in an act of rebellion have we crushed our wonderful Saviour and yet He comes to us with outstretched arms saying, "Father, forgive them for they do not know what they are doing."

The unfailing love of his father brought the prodigal son back home. He had taken great advantage of his inheritance. He squandered his wealth in wild living. Yet when he returned home, his father ran to him, threw his arms around him, and kissed him. David said that the unfailing love of God is his comfort. Knowing that even if we forsake Him, He will never leave us or forsake us brings great comfort. That is His promise to His servants.

As you meditate on this verse, consider the times God has welcomed you back into fellowship with Him.

77. Let your compassion come to me that I may live, for your law is my delight.

In the previous verse, David talked about the unfailing love of God. God's unfailing love is demonstrated through His compassion or mercy. Life itself is a display of God's mercy. Why has God done what He has for you? Is it because you deserved it, or is His goodness to you a pure act of mercy? When I think back to my days before coming to Christ, I cannot come up with a single reason why God should have saved me. I was doing everything exactly the opposite of what one should do to get close to God. My salvation, as well as that of everyone else who has ever lived, is the result of one thing: God chose to have mercy on us. His mercy has come to us for one reason, that we might have life and life abundant.

David said, "Your law is my delight." The word "law" is translated, "teaching." Your teaching is my delight. What does the New Testament teach concerning mercy? Matthew 5:7 gives us a little insight into this matter, "Blessed are the merciful, for they will be shown mercy." God's mercy came to us to give us life. When those who have received mercy show mercy to others, they continue to receive mercy. In other words, those who are life-givers, continue to receive life from God. Having mercy on others is the same as giving others life. It is giving them the very life of God himself, through your kindness.

Can you say with David, ". . . Your law (teaching) is my delight?" Do you delight in having mercy on others? There is a difference between simply having mercy on someone else and delighting to have mercy on someone else. David's delight was to have mercy. If that is not our delight, we are in danger of losing our very lifeline to God. Only those who give mercy receive mercy and only those who delight in it turn it into a lifestyle. "Blessed are the merciful for they shall receive mercy."

As you meditate on this verse, ask God to give you a heart of mercy.

78. May the arrogant be put to shame for wronging me without cause; but I will meditate on your precepts.

David tells us in this verse that even though he has been wronged, he will follow God's instruction. The word "precepts" generally means "instructions." He is describing the essence of spiritual warfare. At the core of spiritual battle is the image a man projects. Satan does not want us to project the image of Christ, that of lowliness and humility. When we are confronted by an arrogant man, Satan wants us to react in kind. He wants us to project the same image as the arrogant man confronting us.

In Matthew 11:12 Jesus is looking for forceful men who can lay hold of heaven or take heaven by force. He then ends His teaching in verse 29 of the same chapter by saying, ". . . Learn from me, for I am gentle and humble in heart. . . ." After calling for forceful (violent) men he says, "Learn from me, I am gentle and humble." The powerful men in the kingdom of God are those who emulate Jesus Christ.

In spiritual warfare, Satan is defeated as we become the opposite of him. We are to never go head to head against him. Pride in the life of someone else cannot be defeated by our becoming more proud than they. This is why a militant foe will never be defeated by a militant church. Jesus is the opposite of Satan in every respect. What David is teaching us in essence is this: the arrogant (the enemy) will be put to shame by our meditation on the precepts of God. Our undying dedication to God will silence all of our critics.

As you meditate on this verse, consider how you react to the arrogant. Do you show them Jesus?

79. May those who fear you turn to me, those who understand your statutes.

Once again David is using his own life as an example for others to follow. All he is saying is, "Follow me, as I follow Christ." In the Old Testament especially, godly men were the only example others had to follow. They were an example of righteousness for others. In the New Testament, Jesus is our example of righteous living. When He left this earth He said, "But I tell you the truth: It is for your good that I am going away. Unless I go away, the Counselor will not come to you; but if I go, I will send him to you" (John 16:7). In verse 10 of the same chapter, He tells us that the Holy Spirit will convict us of righteousness because He (Jesus) is going to be with the Father, where we will no longer be able to see Him.

While Jesus was on earth, He was our example of righteousness but now that He is with the Father, we no longer can see Him. Therefore, He sent us His Spirit to remind us of how He lived. Those who understand His statutes, or those who obey His laws, can now turn to the Counselor for direction as to how to live. The Counselor will convict us as to how Jesus lived.

The Holy Spirit will often use a man who understands the statutes of God as a source of conviction. Those who understand God's statutes and live by them, find that their very lives convict others. So in essence David said, "You who understand the statutes of God, and you that fear the Lord, turn to me. Follow me as I follow Christ." David's very life served as a source of conviction to those who desired to follow God.

As you meditate on this verse, ask God to give you a heart like David's. He was willing to pattern his life after his Lord's so that he could become a living example for others to follow.

80. May my heart be blameless toward your decrees, that I may not be put to shame.

In this verse, David is going through a little heart surgery. To gain a blameless heart, we must be willing to open every aspect of it to God. David had a unique ability to lay himself bare before his God. He understood there was nothing he could reveal about himself that God didn't already know.

In 2 Chronicles 29, Hezekiah has just become king. He was only 25 years old at the time, and yet one of the first things he did was to open the doors to the house of the Lord. The house of the Lord today is in our hearts. We, too, should be willing to open our hearts and say, "God, search me, and know my heart."

Then Hezekiah repaired the doors of the temple. This represents or signifies the subject of forgiveness. The door is the means into the temple. The entryway into the heart (temple) is through forgiveness. When God reveals something to us that is displeasing to Him, we are to ask for forgiveness. This is what repairs the doors.

After he repairs the doors, the priest enters into the innermost part of the temple to remove all the uncleanness he found. Uncleanness signifies a need for repentance. We must first lay our heart out in the open where God can see it. He then will repair the door of the heart through forgiveness so that it will no longer open for sin. He then goes deep within the heart, and with a scalpel, He purifies it by removing all the uncleanness He finds. Repentance! It is one thing to ask for forgiveness, it is another thing to repent of a sin.

Heart surgery has three parts to it. First, we ask God to show us our heart. Secondly, we ask Him to forgive us of every sinful thing He shows us. Thirdly, we repent and turn from our former way of life. Now our heart is blameless!

As you meditate on this verse, ask God to give you a blameless heart.

Kaph

81. My soul faints with longing for your salvation, but I have put my hope in your word.

In this verse, David is expressing the longing of his heart for his salvation. Salvation, in this instance, refers to the complete purification and restoration of his soul, which is what Jesus is and does for us. The intensity of David's desire for it was so great, his own spirit was exhausted. Have you ever been so mentally drained that you felt you might faint? There is a battle being waged over the soul of every man. Satan is constantly attempting to wear down the saints. Sometimes we become weary, and our soul begins to long for Jesus to come and rescue us. "The Spirit and the Bride say, 'Come' " (Rev. 22:17).

David then reassured himself by saying, "But I have put my hope in your word." His hope was in the unmovable Word of God. Though his soul was fainting with longing for Jesus (his salvation), he had not yet found Him. Therefore, he reestablished, in his own mind the basis for his faith. His faith was in God's Word, regardless of what he was facing. Sometimes in our thinking, we believe ourselves to be the center of this life. That is not so! The Word of God stands true, regardless of what we have gone through or are currently experiencing. The Word of God is the center of all things.

When we come to places in life where our soul almost faints with longing for Jesus, where we just can't seem to make it any longer, we need to do as David did. David said, "But I have put my hope in your word." We must take a stand and say, "The Word of God will not fail me." Heaven and earth may pass away but the Word of God will stand forever.

As you meditate on this verse, ask God to give you a heart that is fixed on His Word.

82. My eyes fail, looking for your promise; I say, "When will you comfort me?"

David is obviously going through a very hard time in his life at this point. His eyes now fail him in the same way his soul fainted with longing in the prior verse. He is still looking for his salvation. Initially, he looked with great expectation. However, his eyelids gradually became very heavy.

When I was a boy, I waited in eager expectation for my grandparents to come and visit. They would travel from the opposite side of the state. On the day they were to arrive, I would begin to look for them. I could be found sitting on the couch in front of the picture window, watching every car to see if it turned into our driveway. After a while, my eyes began to fail. I would lose some of my eagerness, but I had looked too long to stop looking.

David had been looking for his salvation (deliverance) for so long he said, "Lord, when will you comfort me?" When will I see Your face, Lord? When will I enter into Your presence? Sometimes the sinfulness of man weighs us down. We become weary to the point that we long like never before to see our Saviour. However, we have no other option but to continue to look for Him. David knew that he needed to keep looking for the promise of God. The heart of David can be heard in the following poem:

> My heartstrings groan with deep complaint;
> My soul lies panting, Lord for thee;
> And every limb and every joint,
> Stretches for perfect purity.

As you meditate on this verse, ask God to help you keep your eyes fixed on Jesus.

83. Though I am like a wineskin in the smoke, I do not forget your decrees.

Years ago in the eastern countries bottles (pouches) were made of skin. In order to have a hot drink, people would hang the pouch (bottle) in the smoke of a fire. With time the outer skin became parched and shriveled. In this verse, David likened the exhausted state of his body and mind to a wineskin in the smoke. David had such a pure heart that he said in essence, "Even though my body and mind are completely exhausted, I won't forget Your decrees."

David did not have a martyr complex. Like any of us, he did not relish his suffering. He wanted deliverance! However, in the midst of his suffering, he learned a great lesson — never give up on God. What hope is there if we become bitter against God? I have heard some say, "God didn't answer my prayer, so I gave up on Him." Do they think their prayer will be answered sooner by giving up on God? David did not forget God's decrees or decisions. He walked as God directed him, even in the midst of suffering. Even in a time where everything seemed to be going wrong, he walked with his God.

The prophet Habakkuk gave us some good advice. "Though the fig tree does not bud and there are no grapes on the vines, though the olive crop fails and the fields produce no food, though there are no sheep in the pen and no cattle in the stalls [you can insert your own dilemma here], YET WILL I REJOICE IN THE LORD, I WILL BE JOYFUL IN GOD MY SAVIOR" (Hab. 3:17-18). The prophet in essence said, "Even though everything on God's green earth is going wrong, I will still rejoice in the Lord." Habakkuk knew, as David did, you never give up on God. We would be wise to follow the apostle Paul's advice in Philippians 4:4, "Rejoice in the Lord always. I will say it again: Rejoice!"

As you meditate on this verse, ask God to help you learn to rejoice in Him even in the midst of trouble.

84. How long must your servant wait? When will you punish my persecutors?

How long must I wait, Lord? When are You going to answer my prayer? Can you relate to those questions? We turn back to the prophet Habakkuk again for some direction. In Habakkuk 1:2 he said, "How long, O Lord, must I call for help, but you do not listen? . . ." Everything was going wrong in the country — there was violence, injustice, and destruction. God was nowhere to be found, or so it seemed. Finally, God answered the prophet with, ". . . Though it linger, [the answer] wait for it; it will certainly come and will not delay" (Hab. 2:3). God's answer to Habakkuk was, "Keep on praying. The answer is on the way, so keep praying for it." In this case, the continuance of prayer was a sign of faith, not a lack of faith.

In Luke 18, Jesus taught us that to persist in prayer is a sign of faith. Because the widow would not stop asking, she finally received justice (Luke 18:5). Jesus ended His teaching in verse 8 saying, ". . . However, when the Son of Man comes, will he find faith on the earth?" He likens faith to those who continue praying against all odds.

Faith is not tested in the answers we get. It is tested in the answers that we don't get. Hebrews 11:39 says, "These (heroes of the faith) were all commended for their faith, yet none of them received what had been promised." Will you still serve God, even though you don't seem to have the answers you are looking for? Faith gives us the ability to lay our life in God's hands. Faith allows us to trust God, even though those who persecute us seem to flourish while we suffer. Faith gives us the ability to die to self.

As you meditate on this verse, ask God if you have the kind of faith that can continue to pray, against all odds, and not give up.

85. The arrogant dig pitfalls for me, contrary to your law.

David is complaining about how the proud recite unholy fables to him, which are not according to God's law. They want David to receive their system of idolatry, and the tales concerning their gods. In the midst of our suffering, we can often become subject to many of "Job's comforters." They offer their advice, but that advice is often contrary to the Word of God. If we follow their advice, it becomes a pitfall, or a trap. There is a great danger in putting yourself into the hands of this world, and discovering what kind of hope we have then.

When Job was going through his troubles, one of his comforters, Bildad, tried to help him through the philosophy of positive confession. Earlier Job had responded to the "comfort" of Eliphaz by saying, ". . . I will speak out in the anguish of my spirit . . ." (Job 7:11). Bildad then says to him, "How long will you say such things? . . ." (Job 8:2). In other words, "Don't be so truthful. How do you expect God to do anything positive while you confess negativism?" Job's response to this was, "If I say, 'I will forget my complaint (become positive), I will change my expression and smile.' I still dread all my sufferings, for I know you will not hold me innocent. . . . you would plunge me into a slime pit . . ." (Job 9:27-31). Job was trying to make them see that if we believe God only responds to positive confessions, we will go into a pit of deception.

Job knew God responds to those who are poor in spirit, those who simply ask. The poor in spirit are beggars who are willing to confess their great need. They understand that asking is the rule of the Kingdom. However, asking is completely contrary to those who are proud in spirit. It's the arrogant who develop pitfalls. The arrogant are proud, self-lovers who are unwilling to confess their true need. They depend upon their deceptive philosophies which keep them entrapped in their own pride, self-sufficiency, and reasoning.

As you meditate on this verse ask God to show you the philosophies in your life that may be contrary to His law.

86. All your commands are trustworthy; help me, for men persecute me without cause.

If we consider something trustworthy, it means we put our trust in it even when we don't have the evidence that it is going to come true. God's commands are trustworthy. A command is an expression of God's will. Not only do they show us what we should do, they also show us what we should leave alone. They direct our life.

David declared a truth concerning God's commands, and then he said, "Help me." It's as simple as that! We don't need to make it any more complex than that. Help me! What more of a cry would a loving parent need from a hurting child? "Help me," is sufficient. No other explanation is needed. Sometimes we think we must "get right" with God before He will help us. That would be like thinking once we are perfect, we are then worthy of salvation. If that were the case, none of us would come to understand mercy. God comes to us when we can no longer help ourselves. If we could pull ourselves out of a pit, there would be no need for the mercy of God. "Help me," could also be interpreted, "God have mercy on me." No other prayer is needed. No other action is needed.

To believe the command, "Be still and know that I am God," means that there will be times when even though we could handle a certain situation, we are to do nothing. We simply put our trust in the mercy of God. When men persecute us without cause, we have many options. We can sue them, we can pay them back and get even, or we can trust in His commands. We must believe that when we are going through a tough time, God is still trustworthy. We must put our trust in what He knows, not in what we understand.

As you meditate on this verse, ask yourself if you really trust in the mercy of God.

87. They almost wiped me from the earth, but I have not forsaken your precepts.

In this verse David expresses how he feels about almost being murdered by his persecutors. However, David's persecutors failed to realize that they could not take the life of one whose entire life was founded in the precepts of God. Instructions for living can be termed "precepts." It's almost as if David is crawling through the desert under a scorching sun and with his last breath saying, "I'm almost gone Lord, but even still I have not forsaken Your instructions as to how I should live." He was under an oppressive spirit and yet he obeyed his God. How many times have we heard "Christians" say, "I've had enough, I know I shouldn't do this, but I can't take it any longer." Then they do something that goes directly against God's instructions to them. David said, "I've had enough, I can't take it any longer. However, I will not forsake God's instructions to me. I'd rather die believing God than forsake His precepts."

In the New Testament, Jesus challenges us to a similar commitment when He responded to the question, "How much should we forgive others. Seven times?" His answer was that we should never stop forgiving others. Even if someone is about to wipe us off the face of the earth, we should still forgive them. David said, "They almost wiped me from the earth." Jesus was wiped from the earth, by us. Yet, while He hung on the cross He said, "Father, forgive them, for they do not know what they are doing." Even in the face of death Jesus would not forsake His Father's precepts.

As you meditate on this verse, ask God to show you where you are quick to forsake His instructions. Then ask Him to forgive you.

88. Preserve my life according to your love, and I will obey the statutes of your mouth.

Throughout this whole section of Scriptures, we see David's life being drained from him. In the previous verse, he described how he was almost wiped from the earth. Now through a simple prayer, his whole situation changes. It is important to note that his enemies were not done away with. Those who persecuted him were still around, but now it no longer mattered because of this simple prayer, "Life me, (preserve my life) according to your mercy."

Satan's name means "destroyer." Jesus means "preserver." In the last seven verses, David's life was being destroyed. In this verse, his life was being renewed when Jesus came in as the Preserver. "Preserve me, quicken me, life me," all mean the same thing. Everything God does, He does unto life. He is the author of life. Therefore, any work of God within us is a work unto life.

David had been going through a judgment. The judgment of God separates evil from good. Therefore, judgment is not negative, it brings life. God judges us unto life. To pray, "*Life* me Lord," is to ask God to remove everything that brings us to death.

David mentioned the proud people who are persecuting him many times. Sometimes the Lord permits people to do outrageously mean things to us, just to get us down (humble ourselves); and if we don't get down, then we don't go through. God did not want David to be a proud man. He wanted him to be humble. In the same way, our life is to be so low that the only life we have is Jesus. It is then that we experience newness of life. Rex Andrews once said, "We are to get so small that we could go through the eye of a needle with plenty of room on each side."[3]

As you meditate on this verse, ask God to "*life* you." Ask Him to bring the very life of Jesus into your soul.

Lamedh

89. Your word, O Lord, is eternal; it stands firm in the heavens.

The Word of God is eternal! It stands firm in the heavens, yet the Word says, "Heaven and earth will pass away . . ." (Matt. 24:35). There are three heavens mentioned in the Scriptures. The first heaven is our atmosphere; it is what we see when we look to the clouds and the stars. The second heaven is Satan's domain. Eph. 2:2 says, ". . . and of the ruler of the kingdom of the air, the spirit who is now at work in those who are disobedient." Satan is the prince of the power of the air. His realm (the second heaven) is not visible to the naked eye, yet is nonetheless real. The third heaven is God's domain. This is what we speak of when we talk of going to heaven one day. Paul referred to this in 2 Corinthians 12:2, "I know a man in Christ who fourteen years ago was caught up to the third heaven." The heavens that pass away are known as the first heaven, our visible world. Therefore the eternal word is that word which is established in God's heaven. This earth will pass away, but the eternal Word of God will exist forever in the presence of God.

The Word one day became flesh and dwelt among us. Now that same Word dwells in us. The same eternal word which will never pass away is dwelling in our very being. That means that you and I who have Jesus Christ, the Word, in us are eternal beings who will live forever in the third heaven, or forever in the presence of God. Heaven and earth may pass away but we never will!

As you meditate on this particular verse, thank God for putting His eternal word in you.

90. Your faithfulness continues through all generations; you established the earth, and it endures.

The earth endures! The earth is the oldest thing man knows. Our bodies came from the earth and will return to the earth. Everything we see, feel, hear, taste, and smell comes from this earth. It is our total, carnal, source. It has endured the flood, fires, earthquakes, hurricanes, tornadoes, drought, and world wars. In spite of all of that, it continues to be the source for all of our temporal needs. The earth has never failed man. Man has failed man, but the earth never has.

It is to this standard (earth) that God likens His faithfulness. His faithfulness continues through all generations. The faithfulness of God is as enduring as the earth. All generations are given the opportunity to partake in His faithfulness. The whole earth is filled with the mercy of God. Every generation from the beginning of time has been given a chance to experience His faithfulness, whether they deserved it or not. So it is not an issue of what we deserve. If we received what we deserved, we would all be lost. It is an issue of the faithfulness of God. Because God is faithful, every generation had an equal opportunity to benefit from it.

His faithfulness is tested through trials. Though the earth has gone through horrendous trials, it always comes through. It always endures. We cannot even relate to the faithfulness of God until we go through trials. In the midst of trials, we must remember the faithfulness of God. His faithfulness will endure.

As you meditate on this verse, think of the faithfulness of God, and how He has always ultimately come through.

91. Your laws endure to this day, for all things serve you.

All things have been appointed to serve God. This verse could also be phrased, "Your laws endure to this day because all things serve You." Our service to God keeps the laws of God alive. God is faithful; because of that we serve Him. Our serving Him maintains the very life of God on earth. If no man served God, there would be no life of God on earth. God lives through and in us. Satan has always sought to destroy true Christianity, for without it there would be no witness of God on earth. However, our humble service to the Lord defeats Satan because it keeps the life of God alive. His laws endure to this very day because men have served God. If all men everywhere served God, this would be heaven on earth.

Servanthood is a position of humility. It is only through humility that the life of God is released from within us. Humility comes through dying to self. In John 12:24 we read, "I tell you the truth, unless a kernel of wheat falls to the ground and dies, it remains only a single seed. But if it dies, it produces many seeds." There is life within the kernel of wheat just as we have the life of Christ within us. However, unless it dies, no life comes from it. The kernel dies in order for its hard outer shell to break open. That hardened shell is representative of our human nature or soul. When that kernel of wheat submits, it opens, releasing life. Likewise, when the human soul submits and dies to its self-centered ways, it opens itself to be filled with service to God, releasing the life of Jesus to others. The presence of God is most powerful when the church service is full of broken people. People who have submitted their will to God keep His laws alive.

The opposite of humility is pride. Pride does not want to serve others, it wants to be served by others. When we want to be served we bring the work of God to a halt. The laws of God endure when men serve God. Even Jesus said, in Matthew 20:28, ". . . The Son of Man did not come to be served, but to serve. . . ."

As you meditate on this verse, consider whether you desire to be served by others or to serve others.

92. If your law had not been my delight, I would have perished in my affliction.

In the previous verse, we saw how through servanthood the law of God endures. We will not even want to serve God until we delight in His law. Moreover, only through servanthood or humility are we able to endure affliction. Without humility, affliction would kill us. When a person loves God enough to serve Him, he places himself in a position of humility. When a man is humble, he endures. He endures because he no longer lives for himself, he lives for his God.

To endure affliction, we must be focused on something greater than ourselves. A parent can endure affliction because of their love for their children. A husband can endure affliction because of his love for his wife. A servant can endure affliction because of his love for his master. David said that if it weren't for his love for the law of God, his affliction would have killed him.

Egocentric people have a terrible time with affliction because it attacks the one thing they love above everything else — themselves. When we were children, we were egocentric. We thought like children. Children think of themselves first and others second. We reasoned like children. The only things that seem reasonable to a child are his own comfort and pleasure. However, when we became adults, we put away childish things. As mature adults, we understand that this life is not about us, it's about Jesus. No longer should we seek presents from God, but rather we should seek the presence of God. Our love should be centered on Him. If we are filled with love for Him, we can endure any affliction because love is patient, love is kind. It does not envy, it does not boast, it is not proud. It is not rude, it is not self-seeking, it is not easily angered, it keeps no record of wrongs. Love does not delight in evil, but rejoices with the truth. It always protects, always trusts, always hopes, always perseveres. Love never fails (1 Cor. 13:4-11).

As you meditate on this verse, ask God to help you put away childish thoughts and reasoning. Make His law the very thing you delight in.

93. I will never forget your precepts, for by them you have preserved my life.

The word "precepts" covers what we generally mean by "instructions." In any position of responsibility, explicit instructions are given for carrying out a person's assigned responsibilities. The same is true of our responsibility for daily life before God. Instructions for living can be expressed as "precepts." The Psalmist states that he will never forget the precepts of God because they are the source of his life. God's instructions to us preserve our life. The word "preserve" is also the word "quicken" or "life." God's instructions bring life to us, which is just the opposite of Satan's instructions which bring death to us.

We are attempting, through this meditation, to understand the mind of Christ. Believing that all Scripture is given under the inspiration of the Holy Spirit, we must also believe that God prompted David to write this because of the spiritual good in never forgetting the precepts of God. "Since, then, you have been raised with Christ, set your hearts on things above, where Christ is seated at the right hand of God. Set your minds on things above, not on earthly things" (Col. 3:1-2).

Would you ever forget the name of someone who saved your life? If a man were to come to your house in the middle of the night and awaken you and your family because your house is on fire, would you forget his name? It's not very likely. Spiritually speaking, the precepts of God awaken us to our great need for God. They life us, or bring life to us. If we are spiritually minded, we too will have the attitude of David and say with him, "I will never forget the precepts of God for they *life* me."

As you meditate on this verse, ask God to *"life"* you according to His precepts.

94. Save me, for I am yours; I have sought out your precepts.

I am yours. That is a term of endearment. I am Yours, O Lord. He who can say this never needs to fear again. In all trials, temptations, dangers, afflictions, persecutions, I am Yours. Is there anything we can face that is bigger than our God? If we are His what can any enemy do to us? Save me, for I am Yours.

In the previous verse, we saw how the precepts of God can bring spiritual life. In this verse, we see them affecting our physical life. Because we are His, we have the spiritual quickening to search out His precepts. David sought out the precepts of God. It is God's instruction to us that literally saves our life from physical dangers.

"It is the glory of God to conceal a matter; to search out a matter is the glory of kings" (Prov. 25:2). It is to God's glory to hide a matter and to ours to search it out. Searching out the precepts of God brings us into more obedience to Him and greater maturity. Wouldn't school have been much easier if the teachers would have simply told us all the answers instead of making us search them out? Where would we be today if we never had learned the benefit of searching out a matter? How would you feel about having a brain surgeon work on you if he had never been required to search out the matter of brain surgery?

It's what we know about the precepts of God through our searching that enables us to live free of fear of our enemies. When we discover something through our own search, that information becomes a part of us. It is quite different from the information we gain through others informing us.

As you meditate on this verse, ask yourself if you are really a searcher or if you are content with gaining other peoples' knowledge.

95. The wicked are waiting to destroy me, but I will ponder your statutes.

The word "statutes" here is better translated "testimonies." Throughout the Bible, the word "testimony" implies the significance of a "witness." The "testimonies" of the Lord are the witnesses which He gives of himself.

How often the wicked wait to destroy us through the lack of a right testimony. We claim Jesus is the way while we aren't satisfied with serving God. We say Jesus is our peace while we fret over what's coming on earth. We say Jesus is love while we can't get along with our neighbor. Through the lack of "witness," the wicked destroy us.

In Acts 1:8 we read, "But you will receive power when the Holy Spirit comes on you; and you will be my witnesses. . . ." The power of the Holy Spirit is to enable us to be witnesses. We often interpret this as meaning the Holy Spirit gives us power to go out and do witnessing. What it is really saying is that the Holy Spirit gives us the ability to emulate the Son of God. Then from within that framework, we may find ourselves witnessing. However, this verse points more to our being than to our doing. Doing religious things is not what's important. Being like Jesus is important. When we cease to be like Christ, the wicked destroy us.

Knowing that the wicked wait for the opportunity to destroy us, we, too, must diligently consider the testimonies (statutes) of God. His testimony, or witness, is that "He is good" and that "His mercy is forever." That must be our testimony also if we have the very Spirit of Jesus living in us.

As you meditate on this verse, ask yourself, "What kind of witness am I? Do I give the wicked ample opportunity to damage the kingdom of God through my lack of witness, or do I hold the enemy back because of my witness?"

96. To all perfection I see a limit; but your commands are boundless.

The literal meaning of the word "perfection" is "human origin." In other words, everything of human origin has its limits and end; but the commands of God are boundless. God's commands know no end. All things human, whether arts, sciences, languages, or inventions, have their limits and end. However, the commands of God, which are a picture of His own mind conceived in His own infinite ideas, transcends the limits of creation.

A command is an uttered expression of a will which is to be obeyed. God imparts His will directly by His commandments. Man's problem is that he often tries to accomplish the will of God through his own means. Our perfection is limited. We can only go so far in revealing God to others. Therefore, we need to be dependent upon God. Whatever God requires of man, He can, by His grace, work in man.

When God told the lame man to take up his bed and walk, the lame man knew instantly there was a limit to his own ability to do so. However, through the grace of God, which is not limited to man's ability, he stood to his feet and walked. Man's ability is limited, but God knows no boundaries.

Have you ever heard someone say, "I've done all I can do!" Many times God will allow us to come to the end of ourselves so we will finally look to Him. At that point God's limitless commands take over and accomplish what we never could.

As you meditate on this verse, thank God for the times He has come through for you when you had reached your end.

Mem

97. Oh, how I love your law! I meditate on it all day long.

Wouldn't it be wonderful if we could live a life of meditating on the things of God all day long? Some would say, "Yes." Others would say, "I'm not so sure." And still others would say, "No!" The key word here is "love." "Oh, how I LOVE Your law!" Not until we love the things of God the way David did will we really be taken up with meditating upon them all day long.

David is expressing first-love desires in this verse. The one with a first-love desire is completely taken up with the one he is pursuing. I remember once when I received a letter from my wife before we were married. I read that letter over and over. Her very words were a comfort to me. I literally meditated upon those words for days. Why? Because I was in love. When you are in love even the words of those you love are important to you. David said, "I love Your law (Lord) so much that I meditate on it all day long."

The word "law" in the Hebrew language means "teaching." It means "law," especially in the sense of the teaching of an authority, whether patriarch, king, or rabbi. In other words, the teaching of the King is law. The Supreme Lord not only utters laws as we think of them, but His utterances are teachings. Whenever Israel backslid, it was because they fell away from the teaching God gave them in His Word. Then when a godly king arose, he was commanded to teach the people how to serve God. So when David expressed he loved the law of God, he was also expressing he intended never to stray from his God.

As you meditate on this verse, examine yourself to see if you really do "love" to meditate on the Word of God.

98. Your commands make me wiser than my enemies, for they are ever with me.

When you meditate on something, it is literally always with you. The commands of God were always with David, making him wiser than his enemies. David was a man of God; therefore, his enemies would have been ungodly men. The fool says in his heart, "There is no God." The wise man believes in God. David's enemies were fools. However, David's obedience to God automatically made him wiser than those who opposed him.

This is not just a matter of intellect. The Proverbs teach us that obedience to God is the pinnacle of wisdom. A man could be highly intellectual without being wise at all. Wisdom is determined by obedience to God. An evangelist was once telling his audience that an average man could take Jesus into his life and gain more wisdom than most highly educated, ungodly men. Suddenly a college student stood to his feet and said, "I believe that is hogwash!" The evangelist thought for a moment and then said, "Sir, I believe you are correct. I have seen the gospel make many pigs clean. In that sense it is hogwash."

Wisdom deals with being instructed by God himself. Daniel was instructed by God, and he was found to have more knowledge than any of the Chaldeans, magicians, soothsayers, etc. Soon his wisdom appeared to the whole nation as being vastly superior to theirs. God instructs us through our obedience to Him.

Wisdom operates only in conjunction with humility. That is why wisdom comes in response to obedience to God. Obedience breeds humility; only the humble obey God. Through the humility obedience produces, wisdom can operate. Were it not for humility, wisdom would turn instantly to pride.

As you meditate on this verse, search your own heart to see if you take pride in your knowledge or if you have a truly humble spirit which simply obeys God. That's wisdom.

99. I have more insight than all my teachers, for I meditate on your statutes.

When the Spirit of God leads you into all truth, you gain more insight than those who merely teach you according to human understanding. In the past two verses, we see David pursuing the law of God, the commands of God, and the statutes of God. David was taken up with the things of God. Subsequently, he has discovered the knowledge of God himself. In Proverbs 2:1-5 we read, "My son, if you accept my words and store my commands within you, turning your ear to wisdom and applying your heart to understanding, and if you call out for insight and cry aloud for understanding, and if you look for it as for silver and search for it as for hidden treasure, then you will understand the fear of the Lord and find the knowledge of God."

Man can help you know *about* God, but pursuing God through prayer can help you *know* God. There is a world of difference between knowing about God and knowing God. Jesus said, "You are in error because you do not know the Scriptures or the power of God" (Matt. 22:29). You are in error because you do not know. Once again we are dealing with the heart knowing, rather than head knowledge. You err because you do not know the Scriptures. This does not mean you have a wrong interpretation of the Scriptures. It means you do not have a knowledge of the one who inspired them. Subsequently, you do not know the power of God; you merely know of it.

To have more insight than your teachers, you must understand the fear of the Lord and find the knowledge of God. That will only come through a pursuit of Him — not a study of Him, but a pursuit. Does your heart throb at the thought of spending time with Him? Can you identify with Isaiah when he says, "My soul yearns for you in the night; in the morning my spirit longs for you . . ." (Isa. 26:9).

As you meditate on this verse, ask yourself if you really pursue the Lord.

100. I have more understanding than the elders, for I obey your precepts.

David spoke more fully about Christ than any who had gone before him. In that sense, he had more understanding than those who were his elders. The Psalms are full of references to the mercy and salvation of God, which describes Jesus. David gained more understanding than those who went before him because he obeyed God's precepts. "Precepts" means instructions. David followed God's instructions. That was the source of his understanding.

The very mysteries of heaven will be opened up to the one who obeys God. Jesus teaches us this in Mark 4:22-23, "For whatever is hidden is meant to be disclosed, and whatever is concealed is meant to be brought out into the open. If anyone has ears to hear, let him hear." First Jesus tells us that all we have to do is hear what God is saying, for God is revealing mysteries. "If anyone has ears to hear, let him hear." You might be saying, "I listen but never hear God." Christ anticipated that. In the next verse Jesus shows us how to sharpen our hearing. In Mark 4:24 we read, " 'Consider carefully what you hear,' He continued. 'With the measure you use, it will be measured to you — and even more.' " In this portion of Scripture, He is talking about spiritual hearing. He first says, "If anyone has ears to hear, let him hear." Then He says, but be careful because the measure of your response to what you hear the first time determines what you hear the second time. The phrase, "With the measure you use," deals with our obedience or response to what we hear. Then He finishes verse 24 by saying, "and even more." In other words, when you hear the Lord speak to you, if you will obey you will hear Him again, but you will hear more. David gained more understanding, or spiritual insight than his elders because he obeyed.

As you meditate on this verse, consider your obedience to God. Can you say with David, "I obey your precepts"?

101. I have kept my feet from every evil path so that I might obey your word.

    The Psalmist walked in the paths that brought glory to God. He did not walk in evil paths, for then he could not live in obedience to the Word of God. The Bible gives us many examples of evil paths. In Romans 13:13-14 we read, "Let us behave decently, as in the daytime, not in orgies and drunkenness, not in sexual immorality and debauchery, not in dissension and jealousy. Rather, clothe yourselves with the Lord Jesus Christ, and do not think about how to gratify the desires of the sinful nature."

    Rather than walking in ways that gratify the sinful nature, clothe yourself with Jesus Christ. I was bothered with an "evil path" some time ago. I had prayed over and over for the release of its grip. One day I decided I was going to have to put on the Lord Jesus Christ instead. I picked out five missionaries to pray for, and then I served notice to the enemy that whenever he tempted me, I would consider that as a reminder to pray for one of those missionaries. I then thanked him (Satan) in advance for the development of my prayer life. The more he tempted me, the more I prayed. Rather than walking in evil ways, I put on Jesus Christ. When we are tempted to walk in an evil path, let that be our reminder to pray. This is how strength is perfected through weakness. Paul had prayed three times for the thorn to be taken from him. Each time God said, "My grace is sufficient for you, for my power is made perfect in weakness."

    As you meditate on this verse, ask God to show you how the weaknesses of your life can be the source of His strength. Then you too, can have the testimony of David, "I have kept my feet from every evil path."

102. I have not departed from your laws, for you yourself have taught me.

The key thought in this verse is that God himself taught David. When the Lord teaches us something, it is not easily forgotten. We have an option. We can either learn through obedience to the Word of God or through the Lord's discipline. When I was a child, my Mom had a phrase she repeated quite often, "Wait till Dad gets home!" That was a dreaded phrase. The rest of the day was spent wondering what his "teaching" would entail.

If we would discipline ourselves to obey the Word of God all on our own, it would save us a lot of trouble. Obedience to the Word through our own discipline was much like listening to Mom when she gave instructions. If you listened, things went along quite nicely. If you didn't listen to her, then you heard that dreaded phrase.

Why was Dad's discipline (teaching) more severe than Mom's? It's not just that he was physically stronger and could spank harder. It's that he represented Jesus in the home. When God has to deal with us because we won't listen to those in authority over us, the discipline is much more lasting. Many times my Dad did not even know why he was spanking me. His anger was over the fact that I didn't listen to Mom. This is what Jesus teaches us in Matthew 21:44 when He says, "He who falls on this stone will be broken to pieces, but he on whom it falls will be crushed." He who falls on the stone is the one who disciplines himself. The one on whom the stone falls is being disciplined by the Lord. When the Lord himself teaches us, we do not soon forget.

As you meditate on this verse, think back to the times when the Lord taught you something.

103. How sweet are your words to my taste, sweeter than honey to my mouth!

The Word of God can be sweeter than honey. Have you ever experienced that? Have you ever heard something from the Lord that was luscious? Proverbs 16:24 says, "Pleasant words are a honeycomb, sweet to the soul and healing to the bones." When words are pleasant, they are received much more quickly. It's not always what is said, but rather how it is said. Whenever the Lord speaks to us it comes from a heart of love. In that light, He could speak words of discipline in an encouraging way.

In Proverbs 16:23, we read of how our own pleasant words can be sweet to those who hear us. "A wise man's heart guides his mouth, and his lips promote instruction." A wise man is a man who fears God. His heart is full of the Lord. When he speaks from his heart, it adds persuasiveness to his lips. When we speak from our hearts, there is a sweetness to our words that make them persuasive because we have an instructed tongue.

Jesus had the same type of tongue. Isaiah prophesies about Him in his book. "The Sovereign Lord has given me an instructed tongue, to know the word that sustains the weary . . ." (Isa. 50:4). Jesus knows how to speak a word in season to the one who is weary. He then proceeds to tell us how He gained an "instructed tongue." "He wakens me morning by morning, wakens my ear to listen like one being taught." Morning by morning, Jesus rose to spend time in the presence of His Father and to be taught by Him. Anyone who spends time in God's presence, being taught by Him, will gain the "instructed tongue" which knows how to speak a word in season to the one who is weary.

As you meditate on this verse, ask God to help you develop the same kind of tongue Jesus had.

104. I gain understanding from your precepts; therefore I hate every wrong path.

I hate every wrong path! Those are the words of a prophet. The prophet is the one known for his "hard" stand on things. For David to say he hates every wrong path means that he is not only talking to the world, but to the Church also. He hated everything that did not bring glory to his God. Romans 12:9 tells us to hate what is evil. Sometimes I think that we tolerate evil rather than hate it. If that is the case, it is because we spend so little time in His presence.

Isaiah hated evil. In his book we read, "Though grace is shown to the wicked, they do not learn righteousness; even in a land of uprightness they go on doing evil and regard not the majesty of the Lord" (Isa. 26:10). Isaiah was crying out for the judgment of God to come down. However, he was not just looking for some type of vengeance. He wanted the majesty of the Lord to be known. In a land of uprightness, or a land where all the people think they are okay, they will go on doing evil. To hate evil is to love God. It is not to hate evil-doers. To love God means you will hate anything that does not truly reflect Him.

To hate evil is to preach against it. If we don't speak out against it, the world and the Church will continue to sin. History shows us that when the Church stops preaching against sin, when it only preaches "love," it gets worse instead of better. If grace is shown on the day when judgment is needed, the wicked never learn righteousness, and they will not regard the majesty of the Lord. David wanted his God glorified. He did not long for judgment, he longed for others to regard the majesty of his God. Subsequently, he hated everything that kept people from seeing who his God really was.

As you meditate on this verse, ask yourself if you really hate evil or if you simply tolerate it.

Nun

105. Your word is a lamp to my feet and a light for my path.

We live in a world of darkness. Without the Word of God there would be no light at all. "In the beginning God created the heavens and the earth. Now the earth was formless and empty, darkness was over the surface of the deep. . . . And God said, 'Let there be light . . .'" (Gen. 1:1-3). The spoken Word of God brought light. Today it is the same. God's Word to us, whether it is spoken or written, is our only source of light.

God brings light to that which is dark. David experienced this first hand. In Psalm 51:6-7 we read, "Surely you desire truth in the inner parts; you teach me wisdom in the inmost place. Cleanse me with hyssop, and I will be clean; wash me, and I will be whiter than snow." God desires truth in the inner or hidden parts of our heart. In Psalm 51 David is confessing his sin of adultery with Bathsheba. God is taking him through a cleansing. The only way for David to be cleansed completely is for him to see his sin. The Word of God was revealing the sin of David's heart, and also lighting a path for him to follow from that point on.

When the revealed Word of God is that which lights our path we will continue moving toward God. God desires truth in the hidden parts of our heart, because our heart is what we follow. When we open our hearts to the Word of God it enters in and reveals all the dark parts.

"Then the Lord said to Moses, 'Pharaoh's heart is unyielding; he refuses to let the people go'" (Exod. 7:14). The word of God came to Pharaoh in the form of Moses, over and over. Pharaoh would not let the word in and subsequently, it hardened. There was no light in it. Pharaoh walked a path that took him farther and farther from God.

As you meditate on this verse, ask God to give you a heart full of light.

106. I have taken an oath and confirmed it, that I will follow your righteous laws.

I have taken an oath. I have made a vow. Those are serious words. Ecclesiastes 5:4-5 gives us some advice in this matter, "When you make a vow to God, do not delay in fulfilling it. He has no pleasure in fools; fulfill your vow. It is better not to vow than to make a vow and not fulfill it." David made a vow and then confirmed it. The only possible way to confirm an oath or vow is through obeying it. David followed the righteous laws of God.

In Proverbs 20:25 we read, "It is a trap for a man to dedicate something rashly and only later to consider his vows." A man is trapped by his own words when he makes a vow. A vow is considered a holy act by the Lord. Even if a vow is made without much consideration (rashly), we are bound to it. I was counseling with a young woman who was determined to leave her husband. I said, "What about your wedding vows?" She said, "Those words didn't mean a thing to me." Whether they meant something to her or not when she made them, the fact remains she made them in the form of a vow and she is bound to them.

Consider the most important vow of your life. You spoke it when you surrendered your life to Jesus. You vowed your life. Philippians 1:6 says, "Being confident of this, that he who began a good work in you will carry it on to completion until the day of Christ Jesus." Through your vow, God began a good work in you and He is not about to leave it unfinished. Our problems begin when we don't want God to complete the work He has begun in us. His completion comes in the form of the refiner's fire. When God starts to refine us we often want out of our vow but we can't get out. God won't let us go for He loves us too much.

As you meditate on this verse, consider whether or not you can identify with David. Have you made a vow and confirmed it, or is God still working with you?

107. I have suffered much; preserve my life, O Lord, according to your word.

It has been said before, but it must be said again. God lifes us. Through praying this 119th Psalm, we are praying the things the Holy Spirit would have us pray. We don't normally think the way God does, so when we see David praying "Preserve my life," we need to take it very seriously and pray it for ourselves. God is continually trying to remind us of our need for Him and that He is our only source of life.

As we go throughout life, we, too, identify with David when he says, "I have suffered much." There is a tremendous price to be paid when you vow your life to God. Saul committed himself to Jesus on the road to Damascus and went from the teachings of the greatest scholars of his time to humble, no-name men who were simply led by the Holy Spirit. Moses vowed his life to God, and was taken from a position of royalty to the desert for 40 years. Joseph was a man with a heart for God and he was sold into slavery. Daniel would not stop praying and ended up in a lion's den. In each case, God preserved their lives.

There is no life outside of God. Our own efforts to better ourselves without God only results in death. David knew firsthand the futility of trying to handle his own life. Some of the things he suffered were from his own disobedience to God. However, some of his suffering simply came from his undying devotion to God. The unique thing about David was he always came back to his source of life. Over and over he says, "Bring life to me, preserve my life, quicken me, life me."

As you meditate on this verse, make that your prayer, also.

108. Accept, O Lord, the willing praise of my mouth, and teach me your laws.

David loved God's presence, which made his praise acceptable to Him. There are true worshipers, and there are false worshipers. There are those who worship God and those who worship worship. John 4:23 says, ". . . The true worshipers will worship the Father in spirit and in truth, for they are the kind of worshipers the Father seeks." The other kind of worshiper, which the Father does not seek, is described in Matthew 15:8-9, "These people honor me with their lips, but their hearts are far from me." They worship Him in vain. Not all worship is acceptable to God.

When we worship a god we no longer pray to, we are false worshipers. David was a man of prayer. Therefore, his worship was acceptable to God. David did not just have a prayer in his life; his life was centered around prayer. David loved the presence of God. Some people say the reason they worship is to enter into the presence of God. Therefore, they feel they love the presence of God. That may not necessarily be true. If you are a worshiper without being a pray-er, then God may view your worship as honoring Him with your lips, but your heart being far from Him. There is a great tendency to worship the feelings worship gives us rather than God himself.

Worship does not bring us into God's presence as much as prayer does. In the Old Testament, God inhabited the praises of His people. Today, God inhabits His people. God lives in us. He is released through our brokenness, not through our praise. The prayer life is meant to break us and humble us. When the humble worship, God is released through their brokenness. Then the sanctuary fills with the presence of God. When the alabaster box is broken then its fragrance fills the room. What we must remember is that prayer is a form of praise and praise is a form of prayer. We must have both in our lives.

As you meditate on this verse, worship Him from your heart.

109. Though I constantly take my life in my hands, I will not forget your law.

Though I constantly subject myself to things that could take my life, I will not forget Your laws. In fact, it is because of those things that I will not forget Your law. Every time we drive our cars, we are taking our life in our own hands. Every time we ride in an airplane, we take our lives in our own hands. We constantly take our lives in our own hands. That can be a wonderful blessing if we allow it to cause us to press in to God. When we know our lives are on the line, we tend to be more serious in our pursuit of God. When our lives are in danger, we tend to remember His law.

The rod and staff represent the law of God. The rod is for correction, while the staff is for strength and direction. When the shepherd needed to bring correction, he used the rod. He did not spare the rod, because he loved his sheep. The staff could be leaned upon when tired or even used as a tool to assist in walking. David learned that the law of God could keep him in relative safety even though his life was in danger. If he allowed it to correct and strengthen him, danger was not so stressful.

David knew the Lord was his shepherd. Because of that, he lacked nothing. He makes him lie down in green pastures, He leads him beside quiet waters, He restores his soul; He lifes him. He guides him in paths of righteousness for His name's sake. Even though he walks through the valley of the shadow of death, even though he constantly takes his life in his own hands, he will fear no evil, for God is with him; His rod (law) and His staff (mercy) comfort him.

As you meditate on this verse, thank God for His life-giving law and mercy.

110. *The wicked have set a snare for me, but I have not strayed from your precepts.*

David is saying, "The wicked are trying to trap me, but if I do not stray from Your precepts (instructions), I have nothing to worry about." The precepts of God are His instructions to us. If we live in accordance with them we do not need to live in fear of what the wicked may try to do to us. In Numbers 23:23 we read, "There is no sorcery against Jacob, no divination against Israel. . . ." There is no direct attack by the enemy that can do anything against the child of God.

If Satan were to come to you and say, "I just want you to know that I will be tempting you real soon to destroy your family and ministry, so beware," you could easily stand against that. That's why Proverbs 1:17 says, "How useless to spread a net in full view of all the birds!" When the enemy lets you know what he is up to, he has defeated his own plan. The only way for the plan of Satan to work is to get our eyes off of the precepts of God. If he can get us to no longer follow God's instructions, then we loose our spiritual insight. Without insight, we can fall prey to his plan.

Listen to the Word of the Lord in Proverbs 1:24-26, "But since you rejected me when I called and no one gave heed when I stretched out my hand, since you ignored all my advice and would not accept my rebuke, I in turn will laugh at your disaster; I will mock when calamity overtakes you." He concludes his thoughts in verse 33, "But whoever listens to me will live in safety and be at ease, without fear of harm."

As you meditate on this verse, ask yourself if you have ever fallen prey to the enemy's plan because of a lack of following God's precepts.

111. Your statutes are my heritage forever; they are the joy of my heart.

In Psalm 119:57 David said, "God is my portion." In this verse, he states he has taken the statutes, or testimonies of God, as his heritage. He is the heir of the statutes of God. He inherited them from his fathers, and he is determined to leave them to his family forever. If a man can leave nothing to his child but a Bible, in that he imparts the greatest treasure in the universe. David was the heir of the testimonies of God. He was the recipient of all that God said he was. What a heritage!

Consider Isaiah's rendering of the heritage of the Lord, "All your sons will be taught by the Lord, and great will be your children's peace. In righteousness you will be established: Tyranny will be far from you; you will have nothing to fear. Terror will be far removed; it will not come near you. If anyone does attack you, it will not be my doing; whoever attacks you will surrender to you. No weapon forged against you will prevail, and you will refute every tongue that accuses you. This is the heritage of the servants of the Lord, and this is their vindication from me, declares the Lord . . ." (Isa. 54:13-15,17).

The great news is that it is our heritage, also. "Now if we are children, then we are heirs — heirs of God and co-heirs with Christ, if indeed we share in his sufferings in order that we may also share in his glory" (Rom. 8:17). We are heirs of the one who is compassionate and patient. If that is His testimony, it is to be ours also. If we are to pass our heritage on to our family, we must have the same testimony as the Lord. What a wonderful heritage!

How will we pass this heritage on? By virtue of being born into His kingdom we become recipients of eternal life. That has to do with me. However, leaving a heritage has to do with my personal obedience to God. I want to leave a heritage for my family, therefore I must live today according to God's statutes.

As you meditate on this verse, thank God for His heritage.

112. My heart is set on keeping your decrees to the very end.

David's heart was fixed on God. To be "set" or "fixed" means to be attached. His heart was steadfast — there was no wavering. No longer was he tossed to and fro, carried about by the wind of every doctrine. He knew his God and that was that. He was determined to obey God right up until the last day, the very end. We live in a day wherein men's hearts are failing them for fear of what's coming upon the earth. If our hearts are not fixed on God, they could fail us also.

David had a unique heart. It seems that from his early days he had a desire for God that others admired. A steadfast heart is not necessarily one which never errs. David had many sins, yet he is not known for them. He is known as a man after God's own heart. That is reflected in his confession of adultery with Bathsheba. In Psalm 51:10 and 17 we read, "Create in me a pure heart, O God, and renew a steadfast spirit within me." "The sacrifices of God are a broken spirit; a broken and contrite heart. . . ."

David's key was that his heart was fixed on God. Even though he sinned from time to time (and these were not small sins), he always ultimately returned to God and said, "Have mercy on me, O God, according to your unfailing love . . . for I know my transgressions, and my sin is always before me." David was always in heart surgery. He knew the central point of his relationship with God was the heart.

Nothing has changed today. The heart is still the central issue. The heart is the home of Jesus. It needs to be pure and it needs to be broken. Those two things develop the steadfast, fixed heart. Blessed are the pure in heart for they shall see God.

As you meditate on this verse, ask God for a pure, steadfast heart.

Samekh

113. I hate double-minded men, but I love your law.

The law of God is our unswerving standard. The law is constant. It never changes. Even in this day of grace, the law remains as it did originally. Jesus said, "I tell you the truth, until heaven and earth disappear, not the smallest letter, not the least stroke of a pen, will by any means disappear from the Law until everything is accomplished" (Matt. 5:18). David loved those whose hearts were fixed upon the law of God. However, for those who wavered, he had another opinion.

James 1:8 tells us that a double-minded man is unstable in all he does. The double-minded man can rest assured that he will receive nothing from the Lord (James 1:7). Why would David use such a strong word as "hate" to describe his feelings for double-minded men? We must recall David's desire to please his God. David was bent on pleasing God. Whenever someone is so motivated, they want others to be, also. Therefore, he hated those who did not desire to please his Lord.

Hebrews 11:6 says, "And without faith it is impossible to please God. . . ." It is from a lack of faith that a man is double-minded. Double-mindedness can be described as someone who asks God for direction concerning something he is facing, and while doing so is figuring out what steps to take when God does not answer him. At the same time he is saying, "God I need Your help," he is figuring out what he can do to answer the prayer himself. He has two minds. He is unstable because his heart is not fixed upon the unwavering law of God.

As you meditate on this verse, ask yourself if you have ever been caught in double-mindedness.

114. You are my refuge and my shield; I have put my hope in your word.

Do you trust God enough to put your hope, your life, or your family's well-being in God's Word? There is no safer place in all the universe than in the hands of our loving God. To place yourself there, you must have trust. There must be enough trust in God to put your hope in what He says. When you do that, He becomes your refuge.

Another term for refuge is the "strong tower." We often read of the strong tower in the Scriptures as the place of safety. The tower was often located some-place in the vineyard where one could run when danger came. The vineyard was a type of church. The keepers of the vines were considered ministers. God was their refuge, their strong tower. They were to go into Him for safety.

In Bible days, the tower was impregnable. With the weapons available in those days, one was completely safe upon entering the strong tower and shutting the door. Though the weaponry of the enemy has changed today (it is no longer arrows and stones, but rather guided missiles and nuclear bombs), our strong tower (Jesus Christ) is just as safe a place as He has ever been. The key is that we must "shut the door." If the door is not shut, the enemy can easily follow us inside.

The door to the refuge is shut through our hope in the Word of God. Isaiah 59:19 gives us this hope, ". . . For he (Satan) will come like a pent-up flood that the breath (Spirit/standard) of the Lord drives along." Another way to phrase this would be, "When the enemy comes in like a flood, the Spirit of the Lord will put him to flight." We stop the flood of the enemy through our hope in God's Word. Through our trust in the Word of God, we shut the door of our refuge to any further satanic influence.

As you meditate on this verse, ask yourself if your hope is securely founded on God's Word.

115. Away from me, you evildoers, that I may keep the commands of my God!

Keeping the commands of God was a theme of David's life. Though we know David was not without his own personal problems, his love for obedience to God was what continually brought him back to seeking his God. He began his book by saying, "Blessed is the man who does not walk in the counsel of the wicked or stand in the way of sinners or sit in the seat of mockers. But his delight is in the law of the Lord . . ." (Ps. 1:1-2). From the very beginning, we have been warned to stay away from evil-doers if we are to keep the commands of God.

An attraction to evil-doers reveals a hidden desire to worship their idols. Evil-doers are all idol-worshipers in God's eyes. They worship the evil they do. When godly men are attracted to them, they set themselves on a path of destruction. Eventually they will no longer keep the commands of their God because to do so would mean to do away with the evil in their lives. Instead they become idol-worshipers.

"What agreement is there between the temple of God and idols? For we are the temple of the living God. As God has said: 'I will live with them and walk with them, and I will be their God, and they will be my people. Therefore come out from them and be separate, says the Lord. Touch no unclean thing and I will receive you' " (2 Cor. 6:16-17). The children of God are the temple of the living God. Therefore, touch no unclean thing. Do not dwell among evil-doers. We are not to have a regular influence of evil in our lives.

Do not mistake this with bringing evil men to Christ. We are to have no intimacy with evil. However, to have contact with evil men for the purpose of winning them to Christ is a totally different thing. This contact is to influence them to receive Christ as their Saviour.

As you meditate on this verse, ask God to show you the evil influences you still have in your life.

116. *Sustain me according to your promise, and I will live; do not let my hopes be dashed.*

No one wants his hopes dashed. If it were not for hope, life would contain no stimulation. However, hope is an interesting subject. Romans 8:24 teaches us, ". . . Hope that is seen is no hope at all. Who hopes for what he already has?" David put his hope in the life that comes through the promises in God's Word. He asked to be given life through God's promises so that his hope would be sustained. We must all live with hope. However, hope that is seen is not hope at all. Hope is a cousin to faith. Faith believes the unseen. Someday our faith shall have sight, but today our faith is in things we cannot see. If we could see, there would be no need for faith. As Romans said, "Who hopes for what he already has?"

Our hope needs a foundation, a basis which is found in the promises of God. Our earthly existence is not as much a basis for life as are the promises of God. This life drains us. God's promises sustain us. Sustain me and I will live. What hope would we have if it were not for the promises of God? "Life me Lord according to Your promise."

Our hope comes from promises like these: "I will never leave you or forsake you," "In my Father's house are many rooms; if it were not so, I would have told you. I am going to prepare a place for you. And if I go and prepare a place for you, I will come back and take you with me that you may also be where I am." Edward Mote was correct when he wrote, "My hope is built on nothing less than Jesus' blood and righteousness; I dare not trust the sweetest frame, But wholly lean on Jesus' name."[4]

As you meditate on this verse, think of a promise God has made to you; therein lies your hope.

117. *Uphold me, and I will be delivered; I will always have regard for your decrees.*

To be upheld, someone must be strengthened and supported. David was asking God to strengthen him and support him for the purposes of deliverance. Our deliverance comes through our God. However, it's not as much a literal, physical deliverance as it is a spiritual one. Consider fear for a moment. Some say fear comes from the unknown. Not true! Fear comes from feeling you need to be your own protector and provider. When a person feels he is responsible for his own protection, the unknown becomes a factor. However, what would a person fear if he walked hand in hand with Jesus? The unknown would not even be a factor. When Jesus supports us and strengthens us, we are automatically delivered from fear. We don't even have to be physically removed from our situation to be delivered.

If a person feels he is solely responsible for his own provisions, he, too, will live in a world of fear, especially in an unstable economy. When he fully realizes Jesus is his provider, his fear leaves. No health care plan in the world can give us the peace Jesus can. When we know Jesus is our strength and support, it removes the pressure that providing and protecting bring.

The New Testament sums all of this up quite nicely in 1 John 4:18, "There is no fear in love. But perfect love drives out fear, because fear has to do with punishment. The one who fears is not made perfect in love." The word perfect means "mature." There is no fear in maturity because the mature person understands God's love for him. Understanding God's love means we understand His protection and provision for us. If a person still lives in fear, it's because his love relationship with the Lord is not what it ought to be. The only way to turn that around is through the daily life of prayer.

As you meditate on this verse, ask God to uphold you.

118. You reject all who stray from your decrees, for their deceitfulness is in vain.

To be rejected means to be downtrodden, or put down. Those who stray from God's decrees are proud people who will not bring themselves under God's authority. In their disobedience they lift up self above God. Ultimately, they will be rejected by God.

"Their deceitfulness is in vain." Proud people often become rich and great by putting others down. They seem to have the world by the tail and appear to be happy, but in reality it is all false. Without obedience to God, one cannot have a clear conscience. Without a clear conscience, there is no true happiness.

A clear conscience comes through our continual pursuit of God. Second Timothy 1:3, speaks about Paul's clear conscience: "I thank God, whom I serve, as my forefathers did, with a clear conscience, as night and day I constantly remember you in my prayers." Paul constantly remembered to pray. His consistency in prayer cleared his conscience.

A clear conscience is a necessity in life, and never more so than in a time of crisis. When we enter a crisis with a clear conscience, we will be able to pray our way through it. However, if we have failed to be constant in prayer prior to the crisis, we will experience great difficulty in our attempts to clear our conscience in the midst of that crisis. First Timothy 1:19 teaches us that if we discard a clear conscience, we shipwreck our faith. Without faith it seems almost impossible to believe God for anything. Nevertheless, the mercy of God overlooks our faithlessness and He even comes to our aid in the midst of our struggles.

As you meditate on this verse, pray this prayer, "Father bring me down." If you pray that prayer, you will never be rejected by God.

119. All the wicked of the earth you discard like dross; therefore I love your statutes.

The Word of God is the only truly pure thing in the world. It is without hidden motive; it is undiluted love. Throughout this Psalm we find David expressing his love for God's Word. In this case, it is God's statutes. In other places David spoke of his love for God's commands, precepts, testimonies, or judgments. David tells us that every facet of God's Word offers a cleansing. The more of God's Word we have in us, the purer we are. The Word serves as a refiner's fire; it removes any dross. As believers, we are to subject ourselves to this fire willingly. To pray for a pure heart is healthy, even though it may hurt us to gain it.

The wicked will not willingly subject themselves to God's refiner's fire. Subsequently, their lives are full of dross. Dross is defined as scum, waste, or foreign matter. Only the pure in heart see God (Matt. 5:8). The wicked have no purity of heart because they will not allow God to inspect their lives. We are wise to openly ask God to inspect our lives and to take us through the fire. The whole idea behind a trial is to purify our lives. The trial is the fire. Before we pass through the fire God works to remove the dross from our lives through His Word. That's where the inspection comes in. Before metal can pass through the fire, the scum at the surface is swept off. If it is not swept off first then it would melt into the metal as it passes through, and would not be pure in the end. Prior to the fire the wickedness of our lives is discarded. That is the inspection or confession process. Then comes the trial or the test to see if we were sincere in our confession. The trial is the final cleansing process.

David said he loved the statutes of God. David realized that through following God's statutes he was preparing (cleansing) himself for any trial that may come his way.

As you meditate on this verse, say with David, "Remove the dross from my life."

120. My flesh trembles in the fear of you; I stand in awe of your laws.

Who can stand in the presence of God? Only the forgiven. It is difficult to fathom that one day we will stand in His presence. It brings a certain chill and wonder to think of that day. However, when that day comes every knee will bow, and every tongue will confess He is Lord. What an awesome day that will be! David said his flesh actually trembled in reverence of his God. David knew that God is a just and holy God and that He requires truth in the innermost parts (Ps. 51:6). God is spirit and those who worship Him must worship Him in spirit and in truth (John 4:24).

The assurance we can gain is through an interest in God's mercy. That alone will save us from the overwhelming fear of one day standing in His presence. Our God is an awesome God, and were it not for mercy, we would have no hope. If the whole earth were not full of His mercy, we would be crushed under the weight of our own sin.

It's from an understanding of mercy that our fear is transformed to reverence. Prior to understanding mercy, one is actually fearful of God. A true concept of God's judgment and mercy creates reverence. Man uses power to destroy and manipulate. God uses power to create. Knowing that God could destroy us with a single breath of His nostril creates a certain fear of God until we fully realize that God is full of mercy. Mercy is a life-giving force. The realization that God could destroy us, but won't, should cause us to bow in reverence to Him.

If we will bow our knee to Him today we will one day be able to stand in His presence. Only when we purposely bring ourselves down or humble ourselves does God lift us up. "Let another praise you, and not your own mouth . . ." (Prov. 27:2).

As you meditate on this verse, thank God for His mercy.

Ayin

121. I have done what is righteous and just;
do not leave me to my oppressors.

Everyone who has the Spirit of Christ in him has a sense of justice. That can cause conflict in our attempts to understand how God deals with us. Justice says, "If I keep up my end of the bargain, you must keep up yours." The problem for us is we feel that God treats us this way, also. Subsequently, we try to earn His blessings. We tend to expect God to be good to us when we have been good. Make no mistake, being "good" is God's objective for us. However, grace sees beyond our actions, forgives us, and grants blessings even when we don't deserve them.

It helps our ego to think we have earned something. It's humbling to receive something we don't deserve. David displayed this mentality when he said, "I have done what is right, therefore deliver me from my oppressors." The Kingdom of God belongs to those who are poor in spirit. The poor in spirit are those who have been reduced to the lowly position of asking (Matt. 5:3).

". . . What does the Lord require of you? To act justly and to love mercy and to walk humbly with your God" (Mic. 6:8). God does want us to live just the way David did. He wants us to do what is right. He wants us to treat others justly. However, our personal motivation should not be that of doing these things so we can get something from God. These things should be a part of our nature now that we have Jesus in us. The reason God delivers us from the oppressor is so we can continue to act justly, love mercy, and walk humbly with our God. God delivers so we can continue to be a blessing to others.

As you meditate on this verse, ask yourself if you do what is righteous and just so you can be blessed, or so your life can reveal the Son of God to others.

122. Ensure your servant's well-being; let not the arrogant oppress me.

This must have been a time in David's life when he was insecure in his relationship with God. He is challenging God to prove himself. "Ensure my well-being," he cries. The Hebrew meaning of "ensure" is to give a pledge or token in times of trouble. The verse could also read, "Be bail for your servant," or "Pledge yourself for me, so I can know that You will pronounce me safe on the Judgment Day."

Have you ever come to the place in your relationship with God where you have said, "God, if I'm going to make it, it will be because of You and not me"? In this verse, as well as the previous one, David is feeling oppressed. He seems to be expressing dismay over how the arrogant are oppressing him. His heart is crying, "Prove to me again that You can keep me, and that You have pledged yourself to me. Be my bail." When the oppressor comes on strong there are times when we sit back and wonder if we really know God.

If you are on a path "into" God, the common thing will be to experience oppression. Whenever God is calling us inward, it seems our world falls apart. Our "world" tends to be something we have created. We have worked hard. We have gained many things. We have a status and a reputation. We know our limits, and we tend to be happy with our world as we have designed it. Then God calls us "into" Him. In order to enter into His world, ours must fall apart. We must see that there is absolutely nothing we can do to gain Him through our design. Our plans, our goals, and our objectives must all die so we can take on His plans, His goals, and His objectives. During that time of death, we fully realize the only reason we are going to make it is because He has become a surety for us.

As you meditate on this verse, think about God being your surety.

123. My eyes fail, looking for your salvation, looking for your righteous promise.

The previous two verses reveal that David is going through a time of oppression in his life. What he speaks of in this verse is typical of us all; we look for deliverance. He is looking for God's salvation, His righteous promise. He feels that he has been looking for so long that his eyes are failing him. David was looking for the Messiah's first coming. We look for His second. It is very much a part of our born-again nature to look for His return. "The Spirit and the bride say, 'Come!' And let him who hears say, 'Come!' . . ." (Rev. 22:17). Come, Lord Jesus!

It is uncharacteristic of a bride in waiting to not live in great anticipation of the groom. It seems in some ways the church has lost the natural characteristics of the bride of Christ. What groom would be content with a bride who does not have a deep longing just to be with him?

Today, we should not look for His return as a deliverance as much as a longing for Him. He is our deliverance already! When troubles come, we go into Him. Much like Noah's Ark, Jesus can carry us through the time of trouble. However, we must go "in." God would like to develop an inwardness in all of us. When our outside world falls apart, we tend to, or at least should, go inward. We tend, in times of trouble, to look at ourselves in a different light. When we look inward, we find Jesus. He lives inside, but He is meek and lowly, and He speaks with a still, small voice. He is not boisterous and aggressive. He must be sought out. When He is found, we will have our deliverance. Since Jesus is already our deliverance, our desires for Him, the crying of our heart and spirit which says, "Come!" should be based on a longing just to be with Him.

As you meditate on this verse, ask yourself if you truly have desires just for Him.

124. Deal with your servant according to your love and teach me your decrees.

We could not hope for a better situation than to be dealt with according to God's love. What could be better than to be in the hands of a loving God? David is beginning to "see" his deliverance here. In the past few verses, he has been oppressed by the enemy but he is now starting to see his way out of it. Often we look for God to pick us up out of a situation and place us on another piece of ground where we will no longer be in it. That may happen one day at His second coming. However, today we still need deliverance. Our deliverance does not come through changing our situation, but rather by changing us.

David prayed, "Deal with me." My situation is not the problem. I am the problem. Or at least, the solution to the problem lies within me. Deal with me. This was an inward prayer. David saw that the things God can accomplish within us are what set us free. Then the situation does not even have to change in order for us to find deliverance. Deliverance comes in the form of God, and God is within us. "Blessed are those who mourn for they will be comforted." The comfort of the sufferer is the Lord himself. When we suffer, we find the Lord in a more real way than we ever do in times of comfort.

Our problem is that we begin to worship our comfort more than our God. When that happens, God removes us from our comfort zones. Then we begin to cry out to God. As all of our comfort fades away, we have no choice but to look within. When we look inside, we find God; hence, our deliverance. God removes the things we trusted in, in order to bring us back to Him. As risky as it may sound, "Deal with me according to Your love," is the safest prayer one could pray.

As you meditate on this verse, ask God to take you inward.

125. I am your servant; give me discernment that I may understand your statutes.

David is asking for discernment so he may understand. Even though the statutes of God are explicit laws, there is more to understanding them than what the intellect can offer. Our intellect gives us one type of understanding, our spiritual life and insight give us another. The Word of God is alive; God lives within His Word. To be properly understood, it takes the Spirit of God. David was being oppressed by arrogant men and he wanted to know the godly way to deal with them.

John 16:13 says, "But when he, the Spirit of truth, comes, he will guide you into all truth. He will not speak on his own; he will speak only what he hears. . . ." The Spirit of God guides us into all truth. Our intellect does not necessarily guide us truthfully. Our intellect is biased. It has preconceived ideas, and when we depend on it wholly, it can lead us astray. The Spirit of God, however, has no bias. He does not speak on His own; He only speaks what He hears the Father tell Him.

To pray for discernment is to ask God to take away any bias we may already have. It is to open our mind to the pure unadulterated Word of God. It is to hear what the Holy Spirit hears. However, to be able to discern, we must have a standard. Discernment is impossible without a norm. Jesus, the Word, is the norm by which we compare or discern. Everything must be measured by who Jesus is. This applies to understanding the statutes of God or discerning the spirit of another person. Discernment is that of comparing what we see in others and what we read in the Bible to who we know Jesus to be. Since Jesus is the standard for all discernment, we need to spend time in His presence. If we fail to pray and read the Word daily, we lose a sense of who He is and what He is like. Hence, we lose the ability to discern because we have no norm.

As you meditate on this verse, ask God to guide you into all truth.

126. It is the time for you to act, O Lord; your law is being broken.

In the previous verse, David prayed for discernment concerning the men who were oppressing him. In this verse, it appears that he received his instruction. He is to do nothing! It is time for the Lord to act! David came to the realization that God will defend His law. The law of God was being broken, and carries its own consequences. David doesn't have to do a thing. God will do it all!

God has established the divine order, or government, by which this universe is run. This order is detailed in His law. When we follow the law of God explicitly, we benefit from our obedience. However, if we fail to obey God's law, government comes into play. Another term for government is that of reaping.

The New Testament equivalent of government is found in Galatians 6:7, "Do not be deceived: God cannot be mocked. A man reaps what he sows." To be disobedient to the law of God is to mock God. Don't be deceived: God cannot be mocked. We will reap what we sow. Deception comes in the form of thinking we are a God unto ourself. That is what the deception of sin is all about. When the serpent deceived Eve, he did so by telling her she would be like God. To be like God would mean we could control the effects of sin. Satan deceives us into thinking that we can sin without it having any effect upon us. He says to us, "One more time won't hurt anything. Go ahead and sin." Paul says, "Don't be deceived, you will reap what you sow because God cannot be mocked." You cannot play God. You cannot control government. David finally came to this revelation and said, "They are breaking Your law. You will act. I don't have to."

As you meditate on this verse, ask yourself if you concern yourself with other people's sin more than you have to, or do you depend on God to deal with them.

127. Because I love your commands more than gold, more than pure gold,

Though this verse is not complete (it continues in verse 128), it makes a very important statement. David considers God's commands to be more precious than gold. He is expressing his understanding of true wealth. The Hebrew meaning for wealth is that of attaining peace of mind. In the first few verses of this section (Ayin), David does not have a peace of mind. He is being oppressed by ungodly men. However, by this verse the Word of God is working in his heart bringing him true wealth. David is discovering that money cannot purchase peace of mind.

David said in essence, "Your commands have given me something greater than gold." Peace of mind. The truly wealthy man is a man of contentment. Peace of mind comes through knowing you are right with God. In 1 Timothy 6, we read about the false doctrine of the love of money. Verses 3-4, say that anyone who gives himself to false doctrine and rejects the sound doctrine of Jesus Christ is conceited and understands nothing. Verse 5 says that his corrupt mind believes that godliness is a means to financial gain. Verse 6 sets us straight when it clearly states, "But godliness with contentment is great gain." Peace of mind is wealth.

Peace of mind will never come through trying to gain control of our life, but rather through giving control of your life to God. Keep in mind that it is the conceited man, the self-centered man, who desires to control others. Money affords us control of ourselves and others. That is why 1 Timothy 6:10 says, "For the love of money is the root of all kinds of evil. . . ." It is evil to desire control of others or even ourself, rather than giving God control of our life.

As you meditate on this verse, ask yourself if you truly love the commands of God more than gold.

128. and because I consider all your precepts right, I hate every wrong path.

The evil path is the one that does not follow God's instructions. "Precepts" is the word "instructions." When God instructs us, we are to follow those instructions explicitly. Wavering from God's instructions is evil. David lived under the oppression of King Saul for many years. He knew first hand that disobeying God's instructions was evil.

God had instructed King Saul in 1 Samuel 15:3, "Now go, attack the Amalekites and totally destroy everything that belongs to them. Do not spare them; put to death men and women, children and infants, cattle and sheep, camels and donkeys." He was instructed to destroy all traces of the Amalekites. In verse 9 we read, "But Saul and the army spared Agag and the best of the sheep and cattle, the fat calves and lambs — everything that was good. . . ." In verses 10-11 we read, "Then the word of the Lord came to Samuel: 'I am grieved that I have made Saul king, because he has turned away from me and has not carried out my instructions.' . . ." God gave explicit instructions to destroy everything that represented the Amalekites.

The Amalekites were very fleshly, carnal people. They represented man's continual struggle with the flesh. If Saul would have completely destroyed them, we would not be so subject to fleshly problems today. However, Saul did not carry out God's instructions completely. His actions were considered so evil by God that He ultimately removed Saul from his position as King. David so loved his God that he literally hated everything that was not in accordance with His precepts.

As you meditate on this verse, ask yourself if you obey God explicitly, or do you have little "insignificant" areas of disobedience in your life?

Pe

129. Your statutes are wonderful; therefore I obey them.

When we consider something to be "wonderful," we often think in terms of it being marvelous or unusually good. God's "wonderful" statutes, in this case, means that they are beyond comprehension. They are too amazing for our mere human minds to comprehend. A statute is an explicit law which is to be obeyed. David is expressing his explicit love and obedience to God by saying in essence, "Even though Your statutes are beyond my ability to understand, they are full of wonder. I will obey them because of my trust in You." Another way of phrasing this is found in the writing of David's son, Solomon, in Proverbs 3:5, "Trust in the Lord with all your heart and lean not on your own understanding."

In Judges 13, we find the account of Samson's birth. An angel appeared to Samson's mother and told her she would have a boy. In verse 8, Manoah, Samson's father, prayed, ". . . O Lord, I beg you, let the man of God you sent to us come again to teach us how to bring up the boy who is to be born." After the angel reappeared and instructed them, Manoah inquired of the angel and said, "What is your name?" In verse 18 the angel replied, "Why do you ask my name? It is beyond understanding." The word "understanding" literally means, "wonderful." The angel replied, "My name is too wonderful for you to even understand." We are not to base our obedience to God on what we understand about God. Who understands God? Do you?

David had a simple love for God that made his relationship with Him something sweet. It was David who said, "My heart is not proud, O Lord, my eyes are not haughty; I do not concern myself with great matters or things too wonderful for me" (Ps. 131:1). The proud man must have everything explained to him before he will obey. The humble man simply says, "God, You are too wonderful for me, I will innocently obey You."

As you meditate on this verse, think of God's wonder.

130. The unfolding of your words gives light; it gives understanding to the simple.

Here is our hope: God gives understanding to the simple. That understanding comes through the unfolding of His Word. God can only reveal to us what we can handle. No man can see God and live. That statement has two meanings. If God were to completely show himself to us in all His glory, before we were ready, it would be our earthly end. God would consume us. Another way to view this is that no man can see God and live the way he has been! A revelation of God would change our lives forever. Saul had one of those experiences on the road to Damascus. He saw Jesus and it blinded him. However, after he regained his sight, he was never the same again.

God has to unfold His Word to us. "Like newborn babies, crave spiritual milk . . ." (1 Pet. 2:2). Babies cannot handle the full revelation of God's Word. The meat of the Word is for those who have learned to chew. "Who is it he is trying to teach? To whom is he explaining his message? To children weaned from their milk, to those just taken from the breast? For it is: Do and do, [precept upon precept] do and do, rule on rule, rule on rule; a little here, a little there" (Isa. 28:9-10). The Lord is teaching those who have been weaned from milk. Even then, He is teaching very slowly. It is line upon line, or unfolding upon unfolding.

We receive revelation according to our capacity to take it in. T. Austin-Sparks once said, "Truth received and not responded to means spiritual declension and loss of capacity." Our capacity to acquire is determined by our response to the truth we have already received. If God speaks to our hearts concerning some area of obedience, and we do not obey, our capacity to receive further truth will diminish.

As you meditate on this verse, ask God to continue to unfold His revelation to you.

131. I open my mouth and pant, longing for your commands.

"I open my mouth and pant," is a metaphor taken from an animal exhausted in the chase. It runs, open-mouthed to take in the cooling air, its heart beating rapidly, its muscular force nearly expended through fatigue. Nothing could demonstrate its earnestness in a stronger way. David sought the things of God with the same intensity one would use to run from a ferocious beast.

David was a shepherd. He had much experience concerning the habits of animals. He most likely witnessed the attack of savage wolves on his flock. He probably observed the graceful deer in need of water. He most likely monitored the hungry hawk as he scanned the earth in a relentless search for food. In all these instances he learned of the determination which drove them toward their goal. He likens these things to his own pursuit of God. He panted after the things of God as an animal in desperate need. He knew his very life was contained in the law of God.

There was another time that David talked about panting. In Psalm 42:1-2 we read, "As the deer pants for streams of water, so my soul pants for you, O God. My soul thirsts for God, for the living God. When can I go and meet with God?" Have you ever prayed, "Lord, make me hungry and thirsty for You — just You"? David had a longing in his heart that puts us to shame. His heart cried, "When can I go and meet with God?" Too often our hearts cry, "When will the prayer meeting be over?"

Martha Wing Robinson once said, "Take all the time you have, all the thought you have, all the energy you have to spare, and follow on to know Jesus, Jesus!"[5] David's cry in this verse was, "I have completely expended myself in pursuit of my God."

As you meditate on this verse, ask yourself if you seek God with a true sense of desperation.

132. Turn to me and have mercy on me, as you always do to those who love your name.

God has mercy on those who love His name. What's in a name? In the name of Jesus, there is everything! There's deliverance in His name, there's healing in His name, and there' s salvation in His name. His name is Wonderful, Counselor, Mighty God, Everlasting Father, the Prince of Peace. To love His name is to love all that it represents, not only for yourself but for others, too. I love the salvation that is in His name, but I love it for others, also. I want others to name the name of Jesus also because of what that name will mean for them. If I desire mercy for others, God will give it to me also.

What will cause God to turn to you and have mercy on you? It will be your desire for others to experience the mercy of God. Can you imagine God turning to you? Can you see yourself standing with the multitudes in heaven worshiping Jesus when suddenly He turns to you and gives you His personal attention? What would cause that? A love for His name!

Isaiah 26:8-9 says, "Yes, Lord, walking in the way of your laws, we wait for you; your name and renown are the desire of our hearts. My soul yearns for you in the night; in the morning my spirit longs for you. When your judgments come upon the earth, the people of the world learn righteousness." The eye of the true prophet sees judgment as merciful. He sees judgment as separation of evil from good. Isaiah goes on to say in verse 10 that if judgment doesn't take place, they will continue to do evil, "And regard not the majesty of the Lord." If the world doesn't understand what the name of Jesus means, they will never regard the majesty of the Lord. Do you want God to turn to you and have mercy on you? Love, respect, and honor His name!

As you meditate on this verse, ask yourself if you have true desires for His name.

133. Direct my footsteps according to your word; let no sin rule over me.

Sin cannot rule over the man whose footsteps are directed by the Lord. An amazing thing happens when a man humbles himself before his God in a renewed determination to obey God. The devil flees. The devil must flee because through humility Jesus comes on the scene. So often we have a mental picture of spiritual battle being that of Satan giving one blow after another to Jesus. Then Jesus musters His strength and answers each blow with a counter blow. That is not so! The battle has been won, the devil defeated.

Satan would like to direct our steps away from God. He would like us to take the easy path where he could then rule over us. However, if we will determine to submit ourselves to God, Satan must flee. James puts it this way, "Submit yourselves, then, to God. Resist the devil, and he will flee from you. Come near to God and he will come near to you . . ." (James 4:7-8). The devil will flee from those who submit and resist. When we take one step toward God, we find that He has already taken a hundred toward us.

If we look at James 4: 6 we read, "But He gives us more grace. That is why Scripture says: 'God opposes the proud but gives grace to the humble.' " Through submission, we resist the devil. Through pride we resist God. If we will walk according to the Word of God, no sin will rule over us because our submission to it brings Jesus. When Jesus is present, the devil flees. There is an amazing freedom over sin that can be experienced by anyone willing to humble himself before God. Typically, humbling comes through confessing your sin to someone and asking them for help. The instant we do that, God gives us grace. If we fail in this, we fail in everything.

As you meditate on this verse, consider whether your life is directed by His Word.

134. Redeem me from the oppression of men, that I may obey your precepts.

The word "redeem" means to liberate by means of payment. The cry of David's heart here is to be set free from the oppression of the spirit of this world. The spirit of this world burdens us through peer pressure. Young people are not the only ones affected by peer pressure. I once read a note to young people that said, "Don't laugh at the way your Dad wears his hair; it's the way all of the people he works with wear theirs. Don't laugh at the kind of car he drives, it's just like his friends' cars. Don't mock Mom for wearing the dress she does, it's what Hollywood is telling her to wear."

The answer to David's prayer has come to us in the form of a Saviour. Jesus liberated us through paying a great price. He came to set us free. We no longer need to worry about the world's "look" and "status" because we are now free of its pressure. This is what overcoming the world means. When I was first saved, I was amazed at the freedom I had to not do what I used to do. The pressure to be like everybody else was gone. I was redeemed.

Paul says, "It is for freedom that Christ has set us free. Stand firm, then, and do not let yourselves be burdened again by a yoke of slavery" [oppression] (Gal. 5:1). Today it seems the Church has gone full circle concerning our freedom. Today the cry is, "We are free to do what the world is doing." Paul warned us of that. We are not free to go back to the same "party spirit" we were saved from. To go back to that is to go back to the oppression of men. "You, my brothers, were called to be free. But do not use your freedom to indulge the sinful nature . . ." (Gal. 5:13). David wanted to be free so he could follow the precepts of God more closely.

As you meditate on this verse, ask yourself how you use your freedom in Christ.

135. Make your face shine upon your servant and teach me your decrees.

Give me a sense of Your approval. Let me know by the testimony of Your spirit, in my conscience, that I am reconciled to You. The godly throughout all ages have derived their happiness from a consciousness of divine favor. The witness of God's spirit in the souls of believers is an essential principle in religion today, as it has always been. The greatest need man has is to know that God approves of him. "Restore us, O God; make your face shine upon us, that we may be saved" (Ps. 80:3). The face of God shines out of darkness. When His face shines upon us, it is a sign that we have passed from darkness to light. When Moses spoke to God face to face, the radiance of God glowed on his face. The glory of God was too strong for others to handle. Therefore, Moses was asked to put a veil over his face. What is the radiance of God? It is Jesus!

Second Corinthians 4:6 tells us, "For God, who said, 'Let light shine out of the darkness,' made his light shine in our hearts to give us the light of the knowledge of the glory of God in the face of Christ." Jesus is the glory of God. To have Him in your heart is to reflect Him in your face. There should be a radiance to our lives. "Those who look to him are radiant; their faces are never covered with shame" (Ps. 34:5). The face that lacks Jesus is a face full of shame. When Jesus shines His face on us, it removes the shame. It causes us to know that one day when we all stand before Him, there will be no shame. "The Lord bless you and keep you; the Lord make his face shine upon you and be gracious to you; the Lord turn his face toward you and give you peace" (Num. 6:24-26).

As you meditate on this verse, ask God to shine upon you.

136. Streams of tears flow from my eyes, for your law is not obeyed.

David was so taken up with his God that he wept when His laws were not obeyed. Have you ever been broken over the broken heart of God? Have you ever wept over the sinfulness of man? The constant theme of David's life was that he had a heart for God. We can often be guilty of weeping over the lawlessness of men, not because they are lost, but because of how their disobedience is making life harder for us. David was concerned about the heart of his God.

In Psalm 6:5-6 we read, "No one remembers you when he is dead. Who praises you from the grave? I am worn out from groaning; all night long I flood my bed with weeping and drench my couch with tears." In these verses, David is weeping over the lost praises of the dead. We often misunderstand the true wealth of worship. David was a worshiper, and he saw it for what it truly is. His tears were shed over those who died without God primarily because God would no longer be able to be praised by them.

Sometimes I think we miss the point when our sorrow for the lost is based simply on their loss. What about God's loss! We are all His children. Ephesians 1:5-6 says, "He predestined us to be adopted as his sons through Jesus Christ, in accordance with his pleasure and will — to the praise of his glorious grace. . . ." Every saved soul is a glorification of His grace. We are the praise of His grace. When a man dies without God, God has lost his praise forever. That is the true tragedy of sin. Once we see the need to bring people to Christ for God's sake, rather than for their own sake, we will find our motives will become much purer in praying for them.

As you meditate on this verse, ask God for a heart like David's.

Tsadhe

137. Righteous are you, O Lord, and your laws are right.

The Lord is righteous, therefore His laws are upright. Righteousness addresses our relationships with men, while godliness speaks of our relationship with God. The man who is righteous is a man who treats men the way God has treated him. Anything you do "in the name of Jesus," is considered an act of righteousness. If you bring someone a drink of cold water because you believe that is what Jesus would do for them, that becomes an act of righteousness.

The righteousness of God is displayed in His treatment of men. God's very nature is that of treating men "right." Therefore, all the laws He has laid down simply line up with His character. Typically, we view laws as restrictions. We believe laws keep us from doing what we want to do. God sees His laws as a protection from harm. They are designed to bring good into our lives. God lives within His Word. You find the life of God in His Word. Outside His law is evil of every type.

In Jeremiah 6, the prophet expressed how those who had left the law of God were in danger. He states in verse 15, "Are they ashamed of their loathsome conduct? No, they have no shame at all; they do not even know how to blush. So they will fall among the fallen. . . ." Because they had left the law of God, they fell into sin. Eventually their conscience became so seared that they no longer even felt shame for their sin. Then Jeremiah called them back to the law of God in verse 16, "This is what the Lord says: 'Stand at the crossroads and look; ask for the ancient paths (laws), ask where the good way is, and walk in it. . . .' " All of God's laws are right.

As you meditate on this verse, consider the fact that all that God does is right for He is righteous.

138. The statutes you have laid down are righteous; they are fully trustworthy.

Continuing on the theme from the previous verse, David now declares that even the statutes of God are righteous. Just as important is the fact that the statutes of God are trustworthy. They are worthy of our trust. A statute is a law laid down, there is no wavering in our obedience to it. The good news is that the statutes are fully trustworthy. It is nice to know that since God has made a statute as something that must be obeyed, He also reassures us that they can be fully trusted.

God is asking nothing more of us than to put our lives in His hands. To put our life in the hands of God is more than just going to church, reading our Bible, and praying once in a while. We are being asked to give up the control we are used to having. We try to maintain control over our lives through things like savings accounts and insurance policies. Though there is nothing wrong with either of those things, they aren't nearly as trustworthy as the statutes of God. When our trust is in temporal things, there is no security in our life even though we have those things for the sake of security.

George Muller was a great man of faith who built several orphanages without ever asking anyone but God for financial help. Late in his life, he was asked once by a young preacher how much he was worth. The young preacher assumed this man of faith must have acquired much in all his years of service to God. Muller was quite disturbed at this, so he reached into his pocket and pulled out a coin purse. Inside were a few meager coins. He looked up and said, "Young man, this is all that I possess in the entire world. My trust is not in this, but in my God."[6] George Mueller was in his nineties at the time, without even the means for retirement, yet he lived with no uncertainty about his future.

As you meditate on this verse, ask yourself if you really believe you can trust your life to God's statutes.

139. My zeal wears me out, for my enemies ignore your words.

David was not only consumed with his God, his zeal was consuming him. He was becoming weary with the lack of attention the ungodly were giving his God. Phinehas was also a man filled with zeal for God. When Moab seduced Israel with the Midianite women, Israel fell into sin. The men of Israel even began to worship Baal. At one time, the sin became so blatant that an Israelite man brought a Midianite woman into Israel's camp. "When Phinehas son of Eleazar, the son of Aaron, the priest, saw this, he left the assembly and took a spear in his hand and followed the Israelite into the tent. He drove the spear through both of them. . . . Then the plague against the Israelites was stopped" (Num. 25:7-8). In verse 11 God says, "Phinehas son of Eleazar, the son of Aaron, the priest, has turned my anger away from the Israelites; for he was as zealous as I am for my honor among them. . . ."

Phinehas was able to turn away God's anger because of his zeal for God. He was as zealous over the honor of God as God was. David had a similar heart. He, too, was zealous over the honor of his God. Do you have a zeal for the honor of God? Are you compelled to see His name glorified? Are you driven to cause others to see the majesty of God? Are you anywhere near being burned-out for God?

John "Praying" Hyde was once examined physically, only to find that his heart had shifted to the right side of his body. His doctor told him that he was too burdened for the work he was doing and suggested that he stop. However, Praying Hyde was consumed with a zeal for the glory of God to shine in India. He never stopped, even though it was literally taking his life from him.

As you meditate on this verse, examine your zeal for God. Do you have any?

140. *Your promises have been thoroughly tested, and your servant loves them.*

The testing referred to here deals with the purifying power of the Word of God. It could read, "Your word is pure" or "Your word is a purification." This is why Jesus said, "You are already clean because of the word I have spoken to you" (John 15:3). It's not saying that the promises are a pure thing (though they are), but rather that they are something that purifies. Your promises have been tested or, I have run Your promises through the fire and find they purify me.

When we are being tested, we put the Word to the test. In the midst of the test (fire), we are being purified by the Word of God. Jeremiah says, " 'Is not my word like fire,' declares the Lord, 'and like a hammer that breaks a rock in pieces' " (Jer. 23:29). In a trial, we often feel as though we have come up against a rock or something immovable. As we cling to the Word of God, it begins to purify us. After purification takes place, the Word then becomes like a hammer that removes the trial (rock). It breaks it into small pieces. As Christ was led into the wilderness to fast and pray, the Word of God was His only sustenance. Later, it became a hammer which crushed His opposition. Every time Satan tempted Him, Jesus quoted the Word.

It's no wonder David loved the promises of God! David was a servant. Servants need tools with which to accomplish their service. The service God's servants perform is the exaltation of God through the defeat of the enemy. Satan is defeated by us becoming the opposite of him. The Word of God is the perfect tool for this task. God's Word is truth. Satan is the father of lies. The way the father of lies is defeated is through the working of truth in our lives. The Word not only purifies us, it also removes that which hinders further service.

As you meditate on this verse, can you say that you love the Word of God?

141. Though I am lowly and despised, I do not forget your precepts.

"Precepts" are instructions. In this case, they are God's instructions to David. David was determined to obey God's instructions even though they caused the world to hate him. David said he was lowly and despised. Lowliness is a love of nothingness. When we willfully give everything to Jesus, we are left with nothing. God keeps taking away and taking away until the only thing we have left is God! Once we have only God, we have everything. However, that state of nothingness is convicting to others because it reveals Jesus. Jesus told us the world hates Him because He testifies that what it does (the world) is evil (John 7:7). Lowliness makes the same statement. He who is lowly is often despised because of how his life reveals Jesus, and the world hates Jesus. However, if we will remain obedient in the face of persecution, we will be saved. Matthew 10:22 tells us this also, "All men will hate you because of me, but he who stands firm to the end will be saved."

He who continues to follow God's precepts, even in the face of persecution, will be saved. Jesus was "despised and rejected by men, a man of sorrows, and familiar with suffering. Like one from whom men hide their faces he was despised, and we esteemed him not" (Isa. 53:3). Yet, in the face of all that rejection, He still followed his Father's instructions and became obedient unto death.

Typically, we are quick to give up doing things God's way when persecution comes. However, if lowliness comes through obedience, and obedience is one of the most effective ways to reveal Christ, what option do we have?

As you meditate on this verse, ask yourself if you have a love for nothingness.

142. Your righteousness is everlasting and your law is true.

Righteousness is everlasting, it keeps on going and going and going. Righteousness never ends; it has an eternal effect on the things it touches. We are eternal beings because of the righteousness of God. Through His righteousness, we have gained eternal life. Now that we have been made righteous, through the blood of Christ, we are called to perform acts of righteousness (Rev. 19:8). Our acts of righteousness have an eternal effect on the ones they touch.

Things that are eternal may not come to pass for some time. We are so prone to thinking in terms of the day we live in that we forget some things may not take effect until the life to come. Consider this. When Moses was walking on this earth doing acts of righteousness, do you think he had any idea those acts would have an effect on us today? When Moses was trudging through the wilderness listening everyday to the grumblings of his people, do you think he had any idea that one day, because of his acts of righteousness, he would appear with the Son of God on the Mount of Transfiguration?

In 1 Kings 17:3-4, we read of when God called Elijah to the desert, "Leave here, turn eastward and hide in the Kerith Ravine, east of the Jordan. You will drink from the brook, and I have ordered the ravens to feed you there." As Elijah was in the desert being fed by ravens, do you think he had any idea that because of his righteous acts, one day he not only would stand with the Son of God on the Mount of Transfiguration, but also be the prophet referred to in the New Testament 30 different times? What is it you may be doing for Jesus today that could have an effect on eternity?

As you meditate on this verse, remember there is more to this life than what you see and hear today.

143. Trouble and distress have come upon me, but your commands are my delight.

Trouble and distress are a part of the normal Christian life. It's not a matter of if trouble will come, it's more a matter of when it will come. If you have the spirit of Christ in you, the world is going to hate you. That alone will cause trouble. The key is not that of avoiding trouble, because it cannot be avoided. The key is that of having delight in God. If we do not delight in God, troubles will overwhelm us.

In the midst of trouble, we typically want to retaliate as best we can so as to relieve ourselves. However, that is the very thing God does not want us to do (retaliate). When we get mad at our God, we want another god, but the command of God says, "You shall have no other gods before me." If your delight is in His command, this one command will keep you from sin. When a teenager gets mad at Mom and Dad, God says, "Honor your father and your mother." If the teen's delight is in the command of God, this one will keep him/her from sin. Right about the time troubles and pressure challenge us to not be quite as committed to the things of God, God reminds us of His command, "Remember the Sabbath, to keep it holy."

Our delight in the commands of God will keep us from sin in the time of trouble. It's during trouble that one seems most vulnerable to sin and temptation. That which pulls us through is our desire to please God. If we delight in His commands, it's because we have a basic desire to please Him.

Meditate on His commands, You shall have no other gods before me, You shall not make for yourself an idol, You shall not take the name of the Lord your God in vain, Remember the Sabbath to keep it holy, Honor your father and mother, You shall not murder, You shall not commit adultery, You shall not steal, You shall not bear false witness against you neighbor, You shall not covet.

144. Your statutes are forever right; give me understanding that I may live.

Understanding is the doing of wisdom. Wisdom is knowledge and insight. Understanding is putting feet to our wisdom. It is the doing, or acting upon what we know. While prayer is the chief thing we do, it cannot be the only thing we do. It is one thing for us to pray for our family, it is another thing to be a godly example in front of them. It is one thing to take our kids to church, it is entirely another thing to go to church with them. The man who has understanding will go with them. He will put to practice the wisdom God has given him.

David was asking for understanding so that he could live according to the statutes of God. Statutes are laws. David knew the wisest thing he could do would be to obey God's laws. Our life comes through our obedience to God. David said, "Give me understanding that I may live!" There is no life in disobedience. Life is found only in obedience to God.

John 10:10 says, "The thief comes only to steal and kill and destroy; I have come that they may have life, and have it to the full." Satan steals life through enticing us to be disobedient. Through disobedience, the life of God is destroyed. Jesus came so we may have life. That life comes through our understanding which promotes obedience.

If you have an area of disobedience in your life, think of how much of life you have been robbed of. A person should counter disobedience with obedience. Every time you are obedient to God, you are taking back the life Satan stole from you.

As you meditate on this verse, ask God to give you understanding so that you may have life.

Qoph

145. I call with all my heart; answer me, O Lord, and I will obey your decrees.

There are several things David did "with all his heart." He followed God with all his heart (1 Kings 14:8), he would praise God with all his heart (Ps. 9:1), he would seek God with all his heart (Ps. 119:10), he would obey God with all his heart (Ps. 119:34), he sought God's face with all his heart (Ps. 119:58), and he kept God's precepts with all his heart (Ps. 119:69). In this verse, he is calling his God with all his heart. What a wonderful quality. This was what distinguished David from others.

David had a pure heart, which is the opposite of a deceitful heart. A pure heart can seek God with all that it is because it has nothing to hide. The heart is who we are. When it is pure, so are we. If the heart is deceitful, so are we. To seek God with all our heart is to reveal the whole heart to God. If there is deceit in our heart, we are hindered in our pursuit of God. In Hosea 10:2-3, we read about the deceitful heart, "Their heart is deceitful, and now they must bear their guilt. The Lord will demolish their altars and destroy their sacred stones. Then they will say, 'We have no king because we did not revere the Lord. . . .' "

The deceitful heart is a divided heart. It cannot focus on God wholly. David was able to give his heart wholly to God because there was no deceitfulness in it. The people in Hosea's day recognized that they had no king because they did not revere the Lord. To do anything unto God with our whole heart is to recognize Him as our KING. David called unto his King with his heart, "Answer me, and I will obey. . . ."

As you meditate on this verse, consider the condition of your own heart.

146. I call out to you; save me and I will keep your statutes.

David is making a new commitment to God because of oppression. In essence, he is saying, "If you save me I will keep your statutes." His call to be saved is not a call for salvation in the sense of being saved from sin, but rather a saving from evil men. Once again, he is being oppressed by evil men. However, oppression may not always be bad if it drives us to new commitments to God.

Proverbs 16:4 says, "The Lord works out everything for his own ends — even the wicked for a day of disaster." "The wicked," or the "day of disaster," can be a part of God's plan for our life. God works everything for His own ends. Everything God does is done to ultimately bring glory to Him. However, God is not seeking glory to quench His ego. It's not that He has a need to be glorified; it's for the good of us. When Jesus is lifted up (glorified), all men will be drawn unto Him. Even the wicked have a role in this. If the wicked can be used as a catalyst to cause man to keep God's statutes, then they play a vital role in the plan of God.

Proverbs 16:19 goes on to say, "Better to be lowly in spirit and among the oppressed than to share plunder with the proud." We are all in the process of taking on the mind of Christ. We don't naturally think as Jesus thinks. Our thoughts are often limited to this life only. God wants us to see there is more than just this life to be concerned about. In this verse, He is telling us just that. In essence, He is saying, "If living among the oppressed will develop lowliness in you, if it will cause you to keep My commandments and statutes, that is better for you than to live the good life with those who don't seek Me."

As you meditate on this verse, ask yourself which is eternally better for you: to live with those who love you, but who never cause you to seek God; or to live among those who oppress you and cause you to seek God?

147. I rise before dawn and cry for help; I have put my hope in your word.

There was a determination in David's life that shames most of us. He had an aching in his soul for the Word of God. Because of the hope he had in God's Word, he would rise early just to hear from Him. David said, "I have put my hope in Your word." The hope of our life lies not only in God's written Word, but also in His spoken Word. Whenever and however God speaks to us, it is a powerful and moving experience.

That which determines whether or not we "hear" from God is our love for the Word. Our love for the Word is tested by our obedience to it. If we are not obedient to it, if we do not have the kind of resolve David had, we will be open to deception.

In Deuteronomy 13:1-4 we read about the power of the false prophet. The account tells us that they can perform miraculous signs and wonders. However, in verses 3-4 it says, "You must not listen to the words of that prophet or dreamer. The Lord your God is testing you to find out whether you love him with all your heart. . . . It is the Lord your God you must follow. . . . Keep his commands and obey him." Those who love God and keep His commands will not be taken in by the miraculous power of the false prophet. This "testing" sorts out the true bride of Christ from those who are simply church-goers.

The "test" of the Lord comes in the form of experiential Christianity versus biblical Christianity. Today, it seems we are trying to prove whether or not something is from God by our experience rather than by the Word of God. If we are a biblically uninformed society, then anything that appears miraculous will be considered to be from God. The problem with this is that not all things miraculous are from God.

As you meditate on this verse, ask yourself if your hope is in God's Word.

148. My eyes stay open through the watches of the night, that I may meditate on your promises.

David had a heart that burned for God. In Psalm 39:3 we read, "My heart grew hot within me, and as I meditated, the fire burned. . . ." David would stay awake throughout the night just to meditate on the Word. And the more he meditated, the more the fire burned. I don't imagine David was able to stay awake all night, every night. However, the challenge before us is: Do we have any sense of fire at all? Have we ever missed any sleep in order to meditate on the Word of God? Do we have a burning within us for God?

David had a fire that guided him through the night. Nighttime and darkness are often equated with times of oppression or trouble — it's when things are not quite as clear as they are in the light. The children of Israel knew of the fire of God, also. In Exodus 13:21 we read, "By day the Lord went ahead of them in a pillar of cloud to guide them on their way and by night in a pillar of fire to give them light. . . ." The children of God were guided through the night by the fire of the Lord. The fire of God will guide us through the darkness of oppression. When we are in the heat of the battle, when we are in the darkest valleys, the fire of God that burns within us keeps us going.

Burn-out comes when we lose the fire. When there is no longer a burning in our hearts for our God, we burn out. There's no flame left. In Exodus 3:2 it says, "There the angel of the Lord appeared to him in flames of fire from within a bush. Moses saw that though the bush was on fire it did not burn up." As long as there is a godly fire burning within you, it will guide you through the night. It will never burn out!

As you meditate on this verse, ask God to put a new fire in your heart for Him.

149. Hear my voice in accordance with your love; preserve my life, O Lord, according to your laws.

If God hears us in accordance with His love, then we can rest assured He always hears us. What a wonderful thought. "This is the confidence we have in approaching God: that if we ask anything according to his will, he hears us. And if we know that he hears us — whatever we ask — we know that we have what we asked of him" (1 John 5:14-15).

God's love is the same as His will. The love of God insists on mercy. The will of God, in all things, is to have mercy. To pray according to God's will is to pray with mercy as the motive. If we pray for anything with the desire for God to be merciful, we pray according to His will. If our heart is sincere, when we pray for God to bless our life so we can continue to bless others, that is a prayer of mercy. If we pray for God to bless our life so we can heap upon our lust, we pray outside the will of God. James puts it this way, "When you ask, you do not receive, because you ask with the wrong motives, that you may spend what you get on your pleasures" (James 4:3). Mercy is our source of life. The mercy prayer is a prayer of life. We have life because God chose to have mercy on us. When we pray asking God to have mercy on others, we are in essence asking God to life that person, or to bring life to that person. When we have a desire for others to have life, we continue to receive life ourself. The merciful continue to get mercy (Matt. 5:7).

David in essence is saying, "Hear my voice in accordance with Your love, and life (preserve) me." When we pray out of a merciful heart, that prayer becomes our very source of life. God will life us. He will put us to life through this simple prayer, "Lord have mercy."

As you meditate on this verse, examine the motive behind your prayers. Do you pray for the sake of mercy?

150. Those who devise wicked schemes are near, but they are far from your law.

The word "law" means teaching. Wicked schemes are the opposite of the teachings of God. Those who devise wicked schemes seem always to be successful. In Psalm 10:2 we read about schemers, "In his arrogance the wicked man hunts down the weak, who are caught in the schemes he devises." The next few verses say the wicked man blesses the greedy and reviles the Lord. Because of his pride, he does not seek God at all. Verse 5 says, "His ways are always prosperous; he is haughty and your laws are far from him." We are often upset at the prosperity of the wicked. However, what would be better: to be prosperous and far from the teachings of God, or to be humble and a follower of God?

To fall into the schemes of the wicked does not necessarily mean our material ruin. However, being far from God's laws will ultimately mean our spiritual ruin. The key is discernment. What it teaches us is that not all material blessings are of God. The wicked are often prosperous. First Timothy 6:5 teaches us that godliness does not always result in material gain. ". . . Men of corrupt mind, who have been robbed of the truth and who think that godliness is a means to financial gain." Godliness only guarantees spiritual gain.

Ephesians 6:11 teaches us, "Put on the full armor of God so that you can take your stand against the devil's schemes." The devil has trapped many spiritually weak people under the guise of material success. This is not to say that material success is always wrong. All the Scripture is teaching us is to put on the whole armor of God so we can discern whether something is of God or of the devil.

David said in this verse that the wicked were near and were often successful from a fleshly perspective, but not from a spiritual perspective for they are far from the law of God.

As you meditate on this verse, determine that you are not going to go the way of all flesh, but will stick to the teachings of God.

151. Yet you are near, O Lord, and all your commands are true.

This is the continuation of the previous verse. In it David said the wicked are near. In this verse he states, "Yet you are near, O Lord," Romans 5:20 put it this way, ". . . But where sin increased, grace increased all the more." When the wicked seem to be overwhelming us, the presence of God becomes all that much more powerful. David put everything into perspective. He said the wicked were near, but they were far from the law of God. God is near also, and His commands are true. The wicked plan schemes which are ultimately false; the commands of God are true. We can put our trust in God's plan.

A command is an uttered expression of God's will, which is to be obeyed. When we obey His commands, we no longer have to live in any fear of the wicked. Some may ask, "Why does God demand so much obedience?" The answer is He wants to protect us from the schemes of the wicked. God doesn't demand obedience so He can show himself as some type of tyrant or mean-spirited dictator. Obedience to Him works to our benefit. It becomes our protection. All the promises of God are conditionally based on our obedience to God. When we come to the full revelation that God's commands are true, we need never live in envy of the success of the wicked.

"You are near, O Lord." David knew the true fountain of life came in the form of God's presence. The presence of God is experienced through following the commands of God. Whether or not we obey God is determined by our love of His presence. Are you content with the presence of God, or must you have more? When you MUST have more, you are in danger of falling into the schemes of the wicked.

As you meditate on this verse, ask yourself how content you are with just the presence of God.

152. Long ago I learned from your statutes that you established them to last forever.

Statutes distinctly mean a law laid down. It means an explicit law. It has to do with the divine order of things. David learned in his youth the need to obey God's divine law. He had gone through many different trials because he did not explicitly obey the statutes of God. Now he refers back to days gone by and says, "Long ago I learned from your statutes. . . ."

As wise as David's son Solomon was, he lacked the heart of his father. David was unique in that his heart was one of conviction. Solomon had wisdom, but not the same conviction his father had. In 1 Kings 3:3 we read about Solomon, "Solomon showed his love for the Lord by walking according to the statutes of his father David, except that he offered sacrifices and burned incense on the high places." The high places are the altars of idols. Solomon did what his dad did. He walked according to God's statutes. However, he would not tear down the high places. He mixed godliness with ungodliness.

Because Solomon lacked the same kind of intensity David had for pursuing God, his heart lacked conviction. He followed tradition. When a person follows tradition, he does things the way Mom and Dad did things. However, he also allows all types of other things in his life because he doesn't have the same purity of heart.

All of Solomon's wisdom could not cause him to develop a heart like David's. David's heart developed out of a love for God and God alone. He was not taken up with lifestyle; he was taken up with the Author of life.

As you meditate on this verse, consider whether you allow a little ungodliness to intermingle with your godliness.

Resh

153. Look upon my suffering and deliver me, for I have not forgotten your law.

In this verse, David is seeking deliverance. He is using his remembrance (practice) of God's law as his premise for asking for deliverance. Obedience is a symbol of love. Our love for God is directly related to our obedience to Him. If a person declares his love to God but does not follow God's law, his declaration of love is considered false by God. We read of this in Ezekiel 33:31, "My people come to you, as they usually do, and sit before you to listen to your words, but they DO NOT PUT THEM INTO PRACTICE. With their mouths they express devotion, but their hearts are greedy for unjust gain." Devotion is measured by our obedience to God, not by our statement of love. It is one thing to tell God how much we love Him; it is quite another thing to live in obedience to Him. Obedience is the measure of love.

In Psalm 34:4 we read, "I sought the Lord, and he answered me; he delivered me from all my fears." Deliverance comes through seeking God, not necessarily from seeking deliverance. We find God in our obedience to Him. Therefore, if we are truly seeking God, we will live in obedience. David is praying, "Deliver me on the basis of my obedience, which signifies my love for You." The presence of God is our deliverance.

The New Testament puts it this way, ". . . God is love" (1 John 4:8). Later in that same chapter John says, ". . . But perfect love drives out fear . . ." (1 John 4:18). Perfect love (God) is what delivers us. It is our love relationship with God that delivers us from fear as well as from suffering. If we live in fear, it's because our love relationship with God is not what it should be. We are not spending adequate time in His presence.

As you meditate on this verse, ask yourself how obedient you are to God.

154. Defend my cause and redeem me; preserve my life according to your promise.

David is saying, in essence, "Defend my cause by redeeming me, which will life me!" If you are a Christian, you have a cause. It is Jesus! There is no other cause we are to give ourselves to, other than this one. The whole essence of the work of God is that we are to reveal Christ to others.

For David to pray, "Defend me," indicates that he has been either imprisoned because of his cause, or that he has charges against him. Jesus paid a price for just one cause; revealing himself to the lost. This one cause will set our society in order. This one cause will bring our nation back to being everything we want it to be. Christ's feelings are so strong about this cause that He was willing to pay any price to redeem us.

The word "freedom" means to liberate by means of payment. Jesus liberated us by means of paying with His own life. He gave His own life to set us free so we could have the liberty to show others the way to freedom. Our redemption is the justification of our cause. Through our redemption, our cause is enhanced. Our redemption lifes us. It brings the very life of Jesus into us.

David prayed, "Redeem me; preserve my life [life me]." We reveal Christ to others through reflecting His likeness. This is the defense of our cause. When we reveal Jesus to others, our cause is justified. The revelation of Christ to a lost world is viewed by the Father as most significant. Any cause that fails to reveal the character and nature of Jesus is pointless. I have witnessed many people standing up for many just causes. However, in the midst of promoting their cause they failed to reveal anything about the nature of who Jesus really is. The revealing of Christ should be the thing that compels us beyond anything else.

As you meditate on this verse, consider whether or not others see Jesus when they see you.

155. Salvation is far from the wicked, for they do not seek out your decrees.

A decree is a decision. In this case it is a decision God has made to give us direction for life. The proof of our salvation is that we live in obedience to God's decrees. However, in order to live in obedience to them we must first seek them out. There is something endearing about seeking something out. To "seek" is to be in pursuit of. To be in pursuit of God's decrees indicates a certain level of love for Him.

The gospel is a love story. It is the greatest expression of love that has ever been displayed. In the Psalms, David is expressing his pursuit of God. However, in the Song of Solomon we see God's pursuit of His bride. God loved us long before we ever loved Him. God was seeking us out before we ever thought of seeking Him. "You have stolen my heart, my sister, my bride; you have stolen my heart with one glance of your eyes . . ." (Song of Sol. 4:9). If you have ever pursued someone, you know how a single glance of their eyes can cause your heart to flutter. We were sought out by God. Just turning our eyes to Him and looking to Him is how we can steal His heart.

If a relationship is healthy, it is mutual. There has to be a seeking on both parts. My father often told me, "Your Mom chased me until I caught her." At the same time God is seeking us out, we are to be seeking Him out. "Salvation is far from the wicked." The proof of that is they do not seek out God's decrees. "In his pride the wicked does not seek him; in all his thought there is no room for God" (Ps. 10:4). The wicked live for themselves. Therefore, there is no pursuit of God. They do not even have thoughts of God.

As you meditate on this verse, ask yourself if you have a true pursuit of God. Do you seek Him?

156. Your compassion is great, O Lord; preserve my life according to your laws.

We gain our life through the law of God because of His compassion. Moses experienced this like no other man has. In Exodus 34 we read the account of Moses receiving the Ten Commandments. God has instructed Moses to chisel out two tablets and to bring them to Him. "Then the Lord came down in the cloud and stood there with him and proclaimed his name, the Lord" (Exod. 34:5). Then He goes into great detail as to what His name means in verses 6-7, "And he passed in front of Moses, proclaiming, 'The Lord, the Lord, the compassionate and gracious God, slow to anger, abounding in love and faithfulness, maintaining love to thousands, and forgiving wickedness, rebellion and sin. . . .' " All of these traits can be summed up in one word, mercy. The compassion (mercy) of God is great!

Prior to this incident, Moses had witnessed God in great power. He watched Him part the Red Sea, destroy his enemies, and lead him through the wilderness by a cloud and a pillar of fire. Now as God calls Moses to the mountaintop, he stands in great reverence and fear as God reveals himself to him. Much to his surprise, he finds that He is not an angry dictator but rather a compassionate, slow to anger, loving God. What relief! What joy! To find out that God (who could have wiped him out with His breath) is full of mercy must have caused Moses great pleasure.

We read of his reaction in verse 8, "Moses bowed to the ground at once and worshiped." What could be more appropriate than that? When Moses found out what the Lord's name means, he bowed down and worshiped Him. Because His compassion is great, because He IS compassion; His laws life us. His law brings life to us.

As you meditate on this verse, worship your great, compassionate God.

157. Many are the foes who persecute me, but I have not turned from your statutes.

"Statutes" are explicit laws. They distinctly mean laws that God has laid down and to which He expects obedience under any and all circumstances. This is especially important in light of what David is facing. He is being persecuted, yet he has not turned from God's statutes. In 1 Samuel 24:4-6 we read, ". . . Then David crept up unnoticed and cut off a corner of Saul's robe. Afterward . . . He said to his men, 'The Lord forbid that I should do such a thing to my master, the Lord's anointed, or lift my hand against him; for he is the anointed of the Lord.'" David knew that even if it meant his own life, he could not turn from God's statutes.

When we are persecuted, we feel quite justified in turning from God's way of doing things. After all, we are being persecuted. This will always be a problem for the person who thinks his life is more important than God's life. David loved his Lord more than he loved himself. Therefore, he could remain obedient even in the face of persecution.

In Communist China an elderly man was persecuted for being a Christian. Since he was also a musician, they took his fingers and sliced them with a razor blade. Then they held them in a fire so he would never be able to play the cello again. In our way of thinking, that would be grounds for retaliation. Listen to the words of this old man: "If I had a thousand hands with a thousand fingers on each hand, I would gladly do it all over again for Jesus. I once used these fingers to bring music. Now I have Jesus and I am music."[7] His life has become a song that all should sing.

As you meditate on this verse, ask yourself how you handle persecution. Do you turn from God's statutes or obey them?

158. I look on the faithless with loathing, for they do not obey your word.

David is expressing his zeal for God in this verse. His love for God's Word is so great that he is disgusted with those who do not obey it. It is easy to relate to the contempt David felt when it comes to those who mock God and His Word.

It is one thing to be zealous for God, it is another thing to be like God. In our zeal for God, we could feel quite justified in loathing those who don't love God. However, if we have zeal without the balance of mercy, we could actually do damage to the work of God as we try to promote it. Proverbs 19:2 says, "It is not good to have zeal without knowledge. . . ." We need a knowledge of what God is like. God is slow to anger, and full of compassion.

Jesus even expressed His disgust with the religious leaders of His day who did not know God. However, the trait we need to pick up is Jesus' immediate forgiveness for anyone, no matter how loathsome they were. Zeal without knowledge is not good. The knowledge we need centers around God's mercy. Without an understanding of mercy, we would stand ready to condemn a person to an eternity without God. Jesus' disgust was based on His love for His Father, not on a hatred for the people themselves. Zeal without knowledge can cause us to hate the sinner rather than the sin. As much as Jesus hated sin and was disgusted with those who mocked His Father, He always stood ready to forgive anyone who sought forgiveness. We can do no less. We must intermingle our zeal for God with His mercy and be ready to lead anyone to Jesus if they express repentance — regardless of how loathsome they may seem to be.

As you meditate on this verse, ask yourself how ready you are to lead the unlovely to Christ.

159. See how I love your precepts; preserve my life, O Lord, according to your love.

"Precepts" generally mean instructions for living. It is God's way of showing us how to live on a daily basis. Instructions are given as to what to do, when to do it, and how to do it. We all have a responsibility of daily life before God. Do you seek Him daily, or read His Word daily, or worship Him daily? David did. Therefore, he could say, "See how I love Your precepts." His daily life was an example of one who loved God's precepts.

In Psalm 90:12 we read, "Teach us to number our days aright, that we may gain a heart of wisdom." This can help us in our daily life before God. Numbering our days aright deals with establishing a list of priorities. Another way to phrase this would be, "Show us the most important thing to the least important thing for us to do today." Through making this a daily prayer, you gain a heart of wisdom because you are developing a lifestyle of giving yourself to the things that God considers the most important.

David then says, "Preserve my life, O Lord, according to your love." Life me, according to Your love would be another way of saying it. This is the third time he has asked God to life him in this section (Resh) of Scripture. The first time, it was according to His promise; secondly it was according to His laws; now it is according to His love. What a wonderful security we have knowing our obedience to God results in God preserving our lives. Jesus is the preserver while Satan is the destroyer. All we need to do is live in obedience to Jesus and our lives are preserved. He lifes us!

As you meditate on this verse, consider your daily life before God. Do you show your love through obedience?

160. All your words are true; all your righteous laws are eternal.

"God is not a man, that he should lie . . ." (Num. 23:19). Every word of God is true. The Word of God is the purest thing we know. It has no bias. It has no mixed motive. It is the way to God, it is the truth of God, and it is the life of God. It is the beginning and the end. Paul said that if we want to find the God of peace, think about ". . . whatever is true, whatever is noble, whatever is right, whatever is pure, whatever is lovely, whatever is admirable . . ." (Phil. 4:8). These things all describe the Word of God and the God of the Word.

There are two facets to the Word of God. There is the written Word of God, the Bible; and there is the living Word of God, Jesus. They are both true. They are the very essence of truth.

In that light, when the Word says that God's righteous laws are eternal, it can be believed. Throughout this section (Resh) of Scripture, we see David going through a time of suffering. He asks God to come to his defense, for he is being persecuted by many foes. He now ends his thoughts by reaffirming to himself that God's laws are eternal. He comes to the realization that if he lives in obedience to God's laws, they will continue to produce good throughout all eternity.

Our obedience to the Word is proof of our belief in it. To say the Word of God is true and to not live in obedience to it is a contradiction. When David states that God's Word is true and that His laws are eternal, he proves it by his obedience to God. These are not trite words, these are the words of David's life. In this section David has prayed three different times, "Preserve my life." He fully recognizes his life comes through obedience to God. James puts it this way, "Do not merely listen to the word, and so deceive yourselves. Do what it says" (James 1:22).

As you meditate on this verse, think about how the proof of your belief in God's Word lies in your obedience to it.

Sin and Shin

161. Rulers persecute me without cause, but my heart trembles at your word.

An earthly ruler or king is a powerful man, at least from man's perspective. It's been said that the president of the United States is the most powerful man on earth. Even though David was being persecuted by powerful men, he understood that only the Lord was to be feared. I have watched men tremble at the prospect of what another man could do to them. David, however, was one who could honestly say that his heart did not tremble at the potential of men, but rather he trembled at the thought of living in disobedience to God's Word.

In 1 Samuel 17 we read of the account where David slew Goliath. In verse 24 it says, "When the Israelites saw the man, they all ran from him in great fear." From man's perspective, Goliath was to be feared. From God's perspective, it was quite another story. David asked, ". . . Who is this uncircumcised Philistine that he should defy the armies of the living God?" (1 Sam. 17:26). David's heart trembled at the Word of God, not the mere challenges of man. Many times we have giants in our lives that dominate us because of our fear of man. Do you respect the Word of God to the point that you would suffer persecution rather than disobey it?

A true story is told of a minister who was put in jail for preaching the gospel in Russia. After 12 years of incarceration, he was told he could go free if he would remain quiet about God for just one week. His reply was, "I cannot accept these terms. What if God tells me to say something to someone before the week is over?" He would not compromise his obedience to God for even one week. He went back to jail because his heart trembled at the Word of God, not at what rulers could do to him.

As you meditate on this verse, ask yourself if you live in fear of men or God.

162. I rejoice in your promise like one who finds great spoil.

David was both a ruler and a warrior. He knew the thrill of collecting the spoil after the battle. Few things could compare to walking through the camp of the defeated to gather up for themselves anything they wanted. However, David knew the true treasures of life were not in the spoil of the enemy but in the promises of God.

Often we are so earthly-minded that we are no heavenly good. I once had an opportunity to be in the same town that was hosting an international triathlon event. The contestants swim for 2 1/2 miles, then they bicycle for 110 miles, and finally they run for 26 miles. They do all this in one day. I learned how one contestant has a regular routine of exercising eight hours every day for this. It is possible in these situations for their body to become their god.

In 1 Timothy 4:8 we read, "For physical training is of some value, but godliness has value for all things, holding promise for both the present life and the life to come." There is nothing wrong with physical fitness. However, it only benefits this life. Godliness on the other hand, benefits not only this life, but also eternity. Physical fitness allows us to gain some of the treasures of this life, but that is all.

The promises of God effect eternity, while the spoils from battle only effect this life. The only time eternal truths truly cause us to rejoice is when we see more than just this life. "Since, then, you have been raised with Christ, set your hearts on things above, where Christ is seated at the right hand of God" (Col. 3:1). What kind of relationship with God would we need to be able to say that God's promises mean as much to us as attaining those things that benefit this life only? We would need a relationship like David's.

As you meditate on this verse, consider what your affections are really set upon.

163. I hate and abhor falsehood but I love your law.

Truth represents God; falsehood represents Satan. The reason we should hate and abhor falsehood is because it is a misrepresentation of God. We should be as absorbed with this as David was. We should literally hate anything that is not a true representation of our God. Sometimes I think we don't fully understand how important this is. What is more important than our God? Who is more important than our God?

Anything that distorts who He is should be hated, especially by those who profess to love Him. The law of God is truth. It leads people to life. Falsehood leads people to death. It is interesting to see how we allow certain falsehoods in our lives as adults, but get very upset when our children allow the same ones in their lives! We often allow the falsehood of this world in our lives. We allow the world to entertain us. We allow worldliness to set our standard of dress. However, when our children begin to reflect some of the things this world stands for, it upsets us as parents. Why is it upsetting us? Because it is a falsehood that is leading them to death. It's leading them to an existence without the presence of God. Too often we tolerate evil rather than hate it.

"Keep falsehood and lies far from me. . . . Otherwise, I may . . . say 'Who is the Lord?' . . ." (Prov. 30:8-9). The attitude here is, "Who does God think He is?" Falsehoods keep us from the truth of who God is. I believe we have lost a true sense of the glory and majesty of our God. We, too, have this flippant attitude of "Who is God anyway?" The influence of falsehoods have convinced us that we can live a wholesome life without fully honoring God. That is a lie and anyone who has believed that lie lives in great danger of eventually not sensing any need for sanctification or holiness. Hebrews 12:14 says, ". . . Without holiness no one will see the Lord."

As you meditate on this verse, ask yourself if you truly understand the glory and majesty of your God.

164. Seven times a day I praise you for your righteous laws.

We do not know whether David literally praised God seven times a day or not. That really is not the issue, anyway. The issue is that he had a priority of praising God for His laws. In Psalm 34:1 we read, "I will extol the Lord at all times; his praise will always be on my lips." Obviously David is expressing a pattern of life in this verse rather than something literal. No one would be able to praise God every waking moment of the day. However, one could become so pleasing to God that their very life becomes a praise to God. In either case, what we find is that David never lost his heart of praise.

In the New Testament, we are encouraged to "pray without ceasing." It would be very difficult at best (if not impossible) to maintain a continual state of prayer. However, it is possible to develop a lifestyle of prayer. It is possible for us to develop a "praying heart" to where prayer is a permanent part of our life. It may not be that of praying every waking moment of our life, but it is that of having a God-consciousness about ourself so that our life becomes more and more a life of praying always.

David had a heart of praise. Seven times a day he would set aside time to praise God for His righteous laws. Throughout this Psalm, the word "law" is used as the translation of the word "teach." David would praise God for the things he was taught by God. The things God teaches us become laws in our lives. To develop a heart of praise, we must purposely praise God for His teachings, also. Do we realize we would not have life if it were not for His laws (teachings)? A person would be wise to read the Proverbs, and each time we find something that gives us advice, praise God for it. If we did this seven times a day, it would change our lives.

As you meditate on this verse, ask yourself if you ever really take time to praise God for His laws.

165. Great peace have they who love your law, and nothing can make them stumble.

Those who love His laws know they are following principles that cannot fail no matter what man may do to him. "You will keep in perfect peace him whose mind is steadfast, because he trusts in you" (Isa. 26:3). We stumble when we are standing on something that is unstable. The one who stands on the law of God will never stumble because nothing could be more stable. When our mind is steadfast, when it is fixed on God, we live in perfect peace. The apostle Paul lived in this same confidence. "Who shall separate us from the love of Christ? Shall trouble or hardship or persecution or famine or nakedness or danger or sword?" (Rom. 8:35). It's not that loving God's law will keep you from trouble, it's that trouble will no longer cause you to stumble in your walk with God because of the peace that comes through loving God's law.

Colossians 3:15 says, "Let the peace of Christ rule in your hearts. . . ." When Paul says, "Let the peace of Christ rule," he is teaching us something very important. The word "let" means it will happen if we don't prevent it. Jesus is called the Prince of Peace, and when He is in our hearts, there is supposed to be a peace that passes all understanding. In fact, peace is the norm for the believer — but we can prevent it if we are not careful. Peace will happen naturally when we love the law of God.

Anything we love, we long to be with. Do we long to study the law of God? Do we diligently search the Scriptures to find His teachings? If we don't do these things, we prevent the peace of God from ruling our hearts. Peace is natural for those who live the normal Christian life.

As you meditate on this verse, consider those practices you have which promote the peace of God in your heart.

166. I wait for your salvation, O Lord, and I follow your commands.

David was looking for the Messiah; his salvation. Today we, too, look for the Messiah, for His return. We are to live with the same kind of anticipation for His second coming as they did who were looking for His first coming. Jesus is coming for those who look for Him. The proof that we are excited about His return is that we live by His commands. His commands are expressions of His will which are to be obeyed.

If there is an area of disobedience in our lives, we lose our desires for His return. I once addressed a group on the soon return of Christ. A few days later I had a number of people call me to complain because I taught that Jesus is coming soon. In each case, the call came from a person who was not living according to all that God commands and who was upset with the thought that He is coming soon. The idea of Christ returning soon is very convicting to those who are living in disobedience to Him.

The Book of Revelation is the most exhaustive material we have on the second coming of Jesus. Near the end of this great testimony we read, "I, Jesus, have sent my angel to give you this testimony for the churches. I am the Root and the Offspring of David, and the bright Morning Star. The Spirit and the bride say, 'Come!' And let him who hears say, 'Come!' . . ." (Rev. 22:16-17). Jesus is the root of David which means David has the heart of Jesus. His heart says, "Come, Lord Jesus!"

David is showing us the true heart of a bride in waiting. The very nature of the bride is one of anticipation. The true bride of Christ has this nature, also. Her heart's cry is that of "Come, Lord Jesus!" She lives with a longing to be with her Groom. She brings her life in obedience to His will. She is taken up with Him!

As you meditate on this verse, give yourself over to expressing your desire for Him to return soon.

167. I obey your statutes, for I love them greatly.

In this verse David prays, "I obey . . . for I love." To obey out of love rather than duty describes submission. It is one thing to obey out of duty. It is quite another thing to obey out of desire. The Pharisees obeyed out of duty. They saw their obedience as something they had no option with. They had to obey to remain a good Pharisee. We must also obey to be a good Christian. However, if we only obey because we feel we have no choice, we simply become a Pharisee.

David obeyed because he loved. David brought himself under God. To love is to give yourself away. To lust is to gain for yourself. David loved (gave himself to) God. He saw his life was not nearly as important as God's. Therefore, he was willing to die to his desires and bring himself under God. Those who "lust" God, are people who obey out of personal benefit. They obey because of how it will benefit them. Those who love God obey because of how it will benefit God.

Make no mistake about it. Our obedience works to our benefit, but we must have a more worthwhile motive than simply our benefit. God doesn't just flippantly design statutes to see if we will obey them. Rather, each one has the express purpose of bringing life to us through obedience. That life is the life of Jesus. The more alive we are with Christ, the more others will see Him and be drawn to Him.

John (Praying) Hyde, missionary to India, had a philosophy on winning souls that was based on the presence of Christ. He felt the only way to draw men to Christ was to emulate Christ. He would spend so much time in prayer that others would see Christ in him and be drawn to him. Whenever he became ineffective in influencing others he would go back to the prayer closet. He knew his effectiveness out in the open came from the time he spent closed in with Christ.

As you meditate on this verse, ask yourself why you obey His statutes.

168. I obey your precepts and statutes, for all my ways are known to you.

Precepts are the instructions God gives us for life. They are the how-to's, the when's, and the where's of life. David said, "My how-to's, when's, and where's are all known to You. Therefore, it would be wisdom on my part to follow your precepts and your statutes rather than my own."

Have you ever put a plan together and then later asked God to forgive you for putting your plan before His? We are full of our own ways. Solomon once said, "There is a way that seems right to a man, but in the end it leads to death" (Prov. 14:12).

David so wanted to follow the precepts and statutes of God that he prayed, "Search me, O God, and know my heart; test me and know my anxious thoughts" (Ps. 139:23). He said, "Show me my heart. Show me the things that are in my heart that are not of You. Show me the plans that I have in my heart that are contrary to Your plans." Then he said, "Test me and know my thoughts." Thoughts have to do with desires. Anything that is a desire of your heart occupies your thoughts. Our "plans" typically evolve out of the thoughts that occupy our hearts. This is why we are to take captive every thought and make it obedient to Christ. When our thoughts (desires) are obedient to Christ, we won't find ourselves doing our own thing.

He then goes on to pray in the next verse, "See if there is any offensive way in me, and lead me in the way everlasting" (Ps. 139:24). An offensive way can be as simple as any "way" that is not in God's direction. It wouldn't even need to be a sinful way for it to be an offensive way. We want to be in the "way everlasting." That "way" is determined by God. All our "ways" are known to God already. All we need to do now is submit them to God.

As you meditate on this verse, commit your "ways" unto Him.

Taw

169. May my cry come before you, O Lord; give me understanding according to your word.

It is most comforting to know that the cry of our heart comes before "... The Lord, the compassionate and gracious God, slow to anger, abounding in love and faithfulness, maintaining love to thousands, and forgiving wickedness, rebellion and sin ..." (Exod. 34:6-7). Can you imagine praying to a god who is anything less than our God? This is what gives prayer its hope. This is our hope of glory!

David's cry is that he would understand according to the Word of God. The Word is God, and God lives within His Word. To gain understanding according to His Word would be to learn how to treat all other people the way God treats us. What understanding would we need other than how to treat our fellow man? We can fulfill the entire law through the simple act of loving God with all our heart, mind, and soul, and loving our neighbor as ourself.

We understand the Word according to our level of love. God is love. To understand His Word we too, must love. "Whoever does not love does not know God ..." (1 John 4:8). If we do not love, we do not need to pray to understand the Word, for there is no understanding outside of love. We must understand love before we will understand judgment, suffering, or righteous indignation.

Without a full understanding of God's love for all, parts of the Word will seem to be a contradiction of itself. God's love is expressed in mercy. Because of God's desire to have mercy on everyone, it becomes entirely necessary for certain "negative" things to happen. However, if those "negative" things ultimately draw us close to God, they are no longer "negative" at all.

As you meditate on this verse, ask God to give you understanding according to His Word.

170. May my supplication come before you; deliver me according to your promise.

In the Old Testament, it was more difficult for supplications to come before the Lord because the standard of the law was an arduous thing to maintain. In Isaiah's day, God was tired of all they were trying to do to find favor with Him. "When you come to appear before me, who has asked this of you. . . . Stop bringing meaningless offerings! Your incense is detestable to me. New Moons, Sabbaths, and convocations — I cannot bear. . . . They have become a burden to me. . . . When you spread out your hands in prayer, I will hide my eyes from you; even if you offer many prayers, I will not listen. Your hands are full of blood" (Isa. 1:12-15). God was tired of their prayers, religious holidays, and sacred assemblies that contained no repentance of sin. It's not so much that these things were that displeasing to God, it's that these things, without repentance, mean nothing to God.

In the New Testament, it is relatively easier for our supplications to come before God because of Jesus. Jesus is the standard by which the law is fulfilled. Therefore, if we have Jesus in us, we qualify for our prayers to go straight to God himself. The only way for Jesus to be in us is through repentance. When a man repents of his sin and receives Jesus, then his prayers gain new life. "Let us then approach the throne of grace with confidence, so that we may receive mercy and find grace to help us in our time of need" (Heb. 4:16). Our confidence is that we are "in Christ." Christ is our confidence that our supplication comes before God. At His throne we find mercy and grace. This is our deliverance. Our deliverance is according to God's promise to have mercy on us.

As you meditate on this verse, thank God for His mercy and grace and that He hears your supplication.

171. May my lips overflow with praise, for you teach me your decrees.

When something overflows, it floods. A flood describes something that is more than enough. David wanted his praise to God to be more than what was necessary. He wanted it to go far beyond just the adequate amount. David always seems to take extreme measures when it comes to expressing his love for God. Often, his life is convicting because when it comes to spiritual things, it is common for us to do just what is required of us and nothing more. We don't typically flood God with anything. We pray just enough to feel good, we give just enough to the poor, and we get upset when the church has more meetings in a week than what we are used to. Not quite a flood!

Even if our lips did overflow with praise, we would never come near that of offering back to God the worship due Him. When we think in terms of "What is the minimal I need to do for God?" rather than "I want to do far more than I really need to," we hurt our relationship with Him. What if a husband's attitude was, "I will provide just the minimal amount for my family," rather than having an attitude that says, "I want far more for my family than just the minimal."

Providing more than enough comes from the heart of God. In Ephesians 3:20 we read, "Now to him who is able to do immeasurably more than all we ask or imagine. . . ." God not only is able to do immeasurably more than we ask or think, He actually *does* more than we ask or think. God not only provides the means for our sins to be forgiven, He removes them, ". . . as far as the east is from the west . . ." (Ps. 103:12). He not only forgives our past, He forgets our past. He goes far beyond just what is necessary. He floods us with mercy.

As you meditate on this verse, ask yourself if your praise of Him could ever be more than enough.

172. May my tongue sing of your word, for all your commands are righteous.

David is praying, "May my tongue sing of your word." The song writer had it right when he wrote, "O for a thousand tongues to sing." Singing the Word of God is one of the ways to tame the tongue. When your tongue sings or speaks the Word, you speak perfectly. James says the tongue ". . . Is a restless evil, full of deadly poison" (James 3:8). Earlier in the same chapter he says that if anyone can tame the tongue he is a perfect man, able to keep his whole body in check.

The only time a man is perfect (mature) is when he never errs with his tongue. When he never errs, he is able to control his whole body. When one sings the Word of God, when his lips are full of praise to God, his tongue is tamed. That is one of the only times you speak without any kind of error whatsoever. When your life is a continual praise, when you sing and speak the Word of God, you gain control of your body because you do not sin as you speak God's Word.

"With our tongue we praise our Lord and Father, and with it we curse men. . . . Out of the same mouth come praise and cursing. My brothers, this should not be" (James 3:9-10).The more we give ourselves over to singing and praising God, the less we will curse men. If we had hearts like David's, hearts that seek God, our lives would be full of praise to God. This would keep us from praising and cursing out of the same tongue.

The reason David sang the Word was because God's commands are righteous. Righteousness has to do with the right treatment of others. When we sing the Word because we love the righteous treatment of men, we no longer curse out of the same tongue. We then use our tongue to bless men.

As you meditate on this verse, consider whether or not you have tamed your tongue through praise.

173. May your hand be ready to help me, for I have chosen your precepts.

This verse could also be read, "I have chosen Your instructions [precepts], therefore I live in complete confidence of Your help, O Lord." What a comforting thought! God's hand is ready to open doors, create opportunities, and nurture those who do things according to His instructions.

The hand of God represents our needs being met, while the face of God represents our relationship with Him. When God encourages us to seek His face, He is wanting us to draw near to Him. His hand is that which is always ready to supply our every need. Often when the people of God became afraid of their situation and how they were going to make it, God would respond to their cries by saying, "Is the Lord's arm too short?" meaning He could still reach His people with all their needs (Num. 11:23). They were not out of reach of God. God's hand can extend to wherever we are with any need we may ever have.

In Matthew 6:31 we read, "So do not worry, saying, 'What shall we eat?' or 'What shall we drink?' or 'What shall we wear?' " These types of worries fall under the care of God's hand. It is the hand of God that provides what we eat, drink, and wear. Then in verse 33 He says, "But seek first his kingdom and his righteousness, and all these things will be given (handed) to you as well." Those who have chosen God's precepts as David did, or those who "seek first God's kingdom" have all their needs met automatically. Those who do not follow His precepts spend all their time worrying about such things.

As you meditate on this verse, ask yourself how much worrying you do concerning the hand of God.

174. I long for your salvation, O Lord, and your law is my delight.

David lived by the law of the Lord, even though he never did see the salvation he so longed for. He lived in anticipation of the Messiah. To prove his dedication, he made the law of God his delight. David is one of those who died in faith, believing the Messiah would one day come. In the great chapter on faith, Hebrews 11, we read, "All these people were still living by faith when they died. They did not receive the things promised; they only saw them and welcomed them from a distance. And they admitted that they were aliens and strangers on earth" (Heb. 11:13).

All of those listed in chapter 11 were completely bankrupt. They were aliens and strangers on earth, they had nothing but faith. They, too, longed for the salvation of God just like David did. In verse 32 and 33 we continue, "And what more shall I say? I do not have time to tell about Gideon, Barak, Samson, Jephthah, David, Samuel and the prophets, who through faith conquered kingdoms, administered justice, and gained what was promised; who shut the mouths of lions, quenched the fury of the flames, and escaped the edge of the sword; whose weakness turned to strength. . . ."

All of these deeds of "faith" were accomplished because of a hope they had for their Messiah. Today we, too, are to live by faith in the same Messiah. Jesus is to be who we long for. Because of deep desires for Him, we keep His law. Even though today we are saved by grace, we still keep the Ten Commandments. Our longing for Him is what purifies us and keeps us on the right path. We have salvation through Jesus. However, we still long for His return. "The Spirit and the bride say, 'Come!' And let him who hears say, 'Come!' " (Rev. 22:16).

As you meditate on this verse, ask God to give you even more of a longing for Jesus.

175. Let me live that I may praise you, and may your laws sustain me.

Let my life be a continual praise to You. David didn't want to praise God once in a while. He wanted his life to be a praise unto God. He says, in essence, "Let me live for the purpose of praising You." He goes on to say that he will gain his life through God's law. "May Your laws sustain [life] me," he cries. David knew the very life of God is contained within His law and that through praise God is enthroned in his heart.

Through keeping God's law, we find the life of God. When we practice righteousness, the very quality of God we display becomes a reality in our own lives. When we are kind to another person, kindness fills our very heart. When we are patient with another, patience fills us. When we are gentle with someone, gentleness fills us to overflowing. The very life, or presence, of God is released through our deeds of righteousness. These qualities are actually the fruit of the Spirit itself. They are the very essence of God himself. Thus, His life, or qualities, sustain us, or life us, as we obey His law. Not only does our obedience to God bring life to us, it brings the life of God to others as well.

Through keeping His law, our very lives become continual praise unto God. There is more than one way to praise God. We focus on the actual verbal praising of the Lord with our lips more than anything. However, your very life itself can become a praise as we reveal God to others through righteousness. Certainly, we want to offer praise with our lips, but we can also praise God with our obedience. David said he wanted to live so that his whole life became a praise unto his God.

As you meditate on this verse, ask yourself how much of your life is a praise unto God.

176. I have strayed like a lost sheep. Seek your servant, for I have not forgotten your commands.

There is a reason why we are called sheep and why Jesus is called the Good Shepherd. Sheep don't have a lot of common sense. If sheep are not led from one pasture to the next, they will continue to eat until there is nothing more to eat. Then they start to eat their own waste. At that time disease sets in. We need to be led. We don't even know enough to stay on the straight and narrow path. We need a shepherd who will continually and gently guide us.

In this verse, David is expressing how we would be naturally lost without a shepherd. He says, "Seek your servant, for I have not forgotten your commands." He says, "Jesus, I love You, I have not forgotten You. However, when I go down the wrong path, seek me out, correct me." He is expressing a complete dependency upon his Shepherd. David is dealing with something that plagues us all; we don't instinctively seek spiritual things. Spiritual desire must be developed. Hebrews 5:14 teaches us that by reason of use, we train our spiritual senses.

Fortunately for us we have a Good Shepherd. Jesus, our Good Shepherd, continually, gently, compassionately, corrects us. How fitting for David to finish this great Psalm with a focus on the One who perpetually seeks us out. " 'Because he loves me,' says the Lord, 'I will rescue him; I will protect him, for he acknowledges my name. He will call upon me, and I will answer him; I will be with him in trouble, I will deliver him and honor him' " (Ps. 91:14-15).

Our Good Shepherd seeks us out. This is the One who deserves all our praise. This is the One to whom we owe our life!

As you meditate on this verse, call on your Good Shepherd to seek you out.

Notes

[1]Carl Lawrence, *The Church in China* (Minneapolis, MN: Bethany House Publishers, 1985), p. 135.

[2]Gordon P. Gardiner, *Treasures of Wisdom* (self-published).

[3]Ofer Amitia, from a teaching (Zion, IL: Zion Faith Homes).

[4]Edward Mote, "The Solid Rock," hymn.

[5]Gardiner, *Treasures of Wisdom.*

[6]Basil Miller, *George Mueller, Man of Faith and Miracles* (Denville, NJ: Dimension Books, Inc.).

[7]Lawrence, *The Church in China.*

Other books by Ron Auch

Pentecostals in Crisis • The Pentecostal movement has been tremendously shaken. It is in trouble, and the world knows it. The media has exposed their dirty laundry for all to see! The "mighty" have fallen for Satan's oldest schemes: sex sin, money, and power. Will this third generation of Pentecostals continue to preach the true "Pentecostal" message? There is an answer, and this book has it! $6.95; Leader's Guide, $2.95

Prayer Can Change Your Marriage • Divorce statistics are growing at an unprecedented rate, and there appears to be no end in sight. Families are being torn apart and lives are being shattered. It's happening in the world. It's happening in the Church. But there is a solution. $6.95

Taught by the Spirit • Even though the Church is emphasizing warfare prayer and actively engaging in what is termed spiritual battle, very little seems to be happening. We are missing what God has truly called us to be because we have become a harlot church. We spend more time worshiping worship than we do Jesus. The spirit of harlotry is running rampant in the Church, thus we are far more fascinated with angels and demons than Jesus himself. $8.95

The Seven Spirits of God • The seven Spirits of God are mentioned four times in the Book of Revelation. What are they, and how do they pertain to us? The seven Spirits of God detail the biblical meaning of being "Spirit filled." God has a definite purpose in wanting His spirit to dwell within men. Peter defined it when he said, "You may participate in the [His] divine nature and escape the corruption of the world." The Spirit of God is to help us overcome the impurity of this world. This book challenges its readers to examine themselves, to see if they emulate all of the fullness of God and are truly living the overcomer's life. $8.95; Leader's Guide, $4.95

Available at bookstores nationwide or call 1-800-643-9535